More Praise for Rich Fettke and *Extreme Success*

"This book shows you how to improve your performance and results while reducing your effort and stress. It is an amazing system that really works!"

—Brian Tracy, author of *Focal Point*

"*Extreme Success* and Rich Fettke's approach are paramount for our times. This is the faster and easier approach for getting what you want."

—Marcia Wieder, author of *Making Your Dreams Come True*

"At last! A book with specific ways for people to enjoy the process of accomplishing their goals. Whether your desire is to improve your income or your life, Rich's ideas are sure to make the path a lot easier. As one of America's top coaches, Rich knows what it takes for people to create Extreme Success without struggling."

—Lee Glickstein, author of *Be Heard Now!*

"Rich Fetttke is an authentic and inspiring communicator. His inside-out approach to success is refreshing and balanced. With his engaging stories and step-by-step approach, Rich shows you how to get the most out of life and have a lot more fun in the process."

—Robin Sharma, author of *The Monk Who Sold His Ferrari*

"The book for the new economy. . . . Rich Fettke is the man to lead folks in this new world."

—Jennifer White, author of *Work Less, Make More*

"An inspiring wild ride! Rich's fresh ideas are just what you need to break old patterns and create the ones you've always wanted. If you want a jolt of inspiration to reach your highest goals, this is your book."

—Susan Harrow, author of *Sell Yourself Without Selling Your Soul*

"Rich Fettke's ability to inspire and lead is nothing short of uncanny, and his gift for helping folks conquer their fears is unsurpassed. Though it's clear he has fire in his belly, there's a rare kind of strength in his soul. His book shows us how to find this strength—and work with others—to easily reach our most cherished goals."

—Michael Gerrish, author of *When Working Out Isn't Working Out*

"Rich Fettke's message is very timely, as the rapid growth of the coaching profession proves. People need to learn how to be better partners in the dance of life and business. Their ability to achieve with ease improves through the power of partnership, and Rich's message is such. It is one the public needs to hear."

—Laura Berman Fortgang, author of *Take Yourself to the Top*

"Rich Fettke is a pioneer in the coaching profession. Being an extreme thinker when it comes to life, Rich is one of those souls who 'lives out loud.' He models in his world what he writes about in this book. A must-read for those who want to break free!"

—DJ Mitsch, past president, International Coach Federation

"Rich Fettke is an inspiring speaker and a leader in the field of personal coaching. Consider yourself lucky to have him as your 'Extreme Success' coach!"

—Talane Miedaner, author of *Coach Yourself to Success*

"Rich Fettke brings a passion and dedication to the realms of learning, coaching, and partnership that are so important to the development of human effectiveness this decade. Rich is most creative and holds a rare and futuristc perspective on the potential of personal success."

—Laura Whitworth, author of *Co-Active Coaching*

"With all the books on self-actualization, I'm delighted to see a book that also shows how our relationships are vital to realizing success in business and in life. Rich is the perfect person to bring these ideas into the marketplace. I can personally attest that, in addition to being a dynamic speaker and masterful coach, Rich Fettke is a leader who inspires both growth and action in individuals and groups."

—Marcia Reynolds, author of *Capture the Rapture*

EXTREME

RICH FETTKE

FOREWORD BY RICHARD CARLSON, PH.D.,

author of *Don't Sweat the Small Stuff...and it's all small stuff*

A FIRESIDE BOOK

PUBLISHED BY SIMON & SCHUSTER

New York   London   Toronto   Sydney   Singapore

EXTREME SUCCESS

The 7-Part Program

That Shows You How to

Succeed Without

Struggle

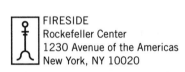
FIRESIDE
Rockefeller Center
1230 Avenue of the Americas
New York, NY 10020

FIRESIDE and colophon are registered trademarks
of Simon & Schuster, Inc.

For information about special discounts for bulk purchases,
please contact Simon & Schuster Special Sales:
1-800-456-6798 or business@simonandschuster.com

Designed by Katy Riegel

Manufactured in the United States of America

10   9   8   7   6   5   4   3   2   1

Library of Congress Cataloging-in-Publication Data is available.

ISBN 0-7432-2314-4 (Pbk.)
     0-7432-2953-3

Acknowledgments

There are so many people I am grateful to have in my life, and being able to say thank you to them in this book is a blessing. As I write these acknowledgments, I'm presented with the challenge of keeping this section from doubling the size of this book. So, for all of you who have been with me on this journey, and whom I have not personally thanked in the following paragraphs, please know that I appreciate you more than you can imagine.

First of all, Caroline Sutton, my editor at Simon & Schuster, deserves a high five and a big hug. Thank you, Caroline, for seeing the vision and for your constant encouragement. You are my ideal editor! Also, thanks to the rest of the "Extreme Success Team" at Simon & Schuster: Mark Gompertz, Nicole Diamond, Marcia Burch, Chris Lloreda, Debbie Model, Trish Todd, Chris Lynch, Cherlynne Li, and the S&S sales force. You've all been extremely helpful, and you've kept the publishing process exciting and fun.

Thanks to my gifted agent, David Hale Smith, the prez of DHS Literary, for being one of my greatest fans and for knowing how to "work it" with amazing confidence. You're an ideal agent and an awesome friend. Also, thanks to Seth,

Courtney, Elizabeth, Phoebe, and Charlotte for being part of the DHS team. I appreciate you all.

My parents, John and Mari Fettke, are amazing people. Thank you for how well you handled me as a "hyperkinetic" kid and for always holding the belief that someday I'd channel that energy toward something positive. Words cannot express how much I appreciate and love you.

I am incredibly grateful for my parents-in-law, Doug and Barbara Morrison. I appreciate all that you have given me. You're the best!

Thank you to my younger brother, Steve Fettke, for all the adrenaline rushes we've shared. Also, thank you to Steve's wife, Kimi Fettke, my older brother, Rob Fettke, and his wife, Karen VonKoeckritz. I greatly appreciate your encouragement and support.

And thank you my ever-expanding family—the Morrisons, Conways, Winklers, Hickeys, Sampsons, and the Arfanises. Also, a special thank you to Tom Vitale, for trusting and accepting me as Karina's "Papa."

Nana, I did it! Thank you for inspiring me to continually educate myself and grow and to take the "high road" in life. I feel your presence.

My workout partner and climbing bud, Jim "Bolt" Cope, is always there to hold me accountable and to keep me in the Zone with the weights and on the rock. Thank you, Jimbo. I am very, very grateful for our partnership and our friendship.

My Success Partner and friend, Gerald "G" Guintu, is there every week to hold me accountable, to acknowledge me, and to keep things fun and exciting. Thanks, Brah! You're my soul brother.

Thank you to Dave "Dazey" Kelleher for being such a loving and authentic friend. I am so glad that you moved to Cal with me! You have the heart of an eagle!

To Cheryl Richardson and Michael Gerrish, two of the most loving, authentic, and generous people I have ever met. I owe you both some major "duty" for helping me turn this book from a dream into reality. Thank you so much. I love you guys!

A big hug to Richard Carlson for writing a wonderful foreword for this book and for showing me that no matter how successful a person becomes, he can still be incredibly giving, loving, and real. Thank you for your support and for constantly walking your talk. Also, many thanks to Richard's amazing assistant, Nicole Walton, and to his former assistant (and fantastic author and speaker) Rhonda Hull.

The incredible "wordsmith" Susan Suffes helped me create a powerful book proposal and was my writing partner day after day after day until my manuscript was ready to hand in to Simon & Schuster. Thank you, Susan, for making the process struggle-free!

My personal coach, Cynthia Loy Darst, for helping me wake up and realize that the struggle is not noble. Thank you, CLD! You've helped me strengthen my emotional courage.

I have a huge amount of gratitude for the following folks who have contributed to this book and to my life: Jane Atkinson and the fantastic folks at International Speakers Bureau, Dr. John Pagano, Kate Douglas, Vickie Sullivan, Susan Harrow, Richard Toronto, Lisa Keating, the National Speakers Association and the Northern California Chapter of the NSA, Laura Whitworth, Henry Kimsey-House, Karen Kimsey-House and all the co-active leaders at the Coaches Training Institute, Laura Berman Fortgang, PSI Seminars, Mark and Susan Lamb, Marcia Wieder, Lee Glickstein, Talane Miedaner, Jennifer White, Robin Sharma, Brian Tracy, Bob Davies, Virgil Beasley, Mike Lantz, Tamara Gerlack, Julie Tiffee, and all the altitude addicts at Bay Area Skydiving.

Many thanks for all the encouragement and love from my California Crew: Jill Wagner, Jeanna Gabellini, Brandon and Kimberly Barrett, Chuck Diguida, Tim Ennis, Randy and Corbie Baugh, Boomer Angove, Jen Moseley, Dondra Nickell, JJ Gabellini, Mandy Birks, Andrea Gaspari, Michael Chevrolotti, Neil Brito, Steve Ferro, and Brad LeCraw. Having you all in my life is true ecstasy.

Thank you from the bottom of my heart to the International Coach Federation for the unending support of my career and for building, supporting, and growing the integrity of the coaching profession. An extra big hug to Jeff Raim, John Sieffer, Marcia Reynolds, DJ Mitsch, and Bobette Reeder.

My clients have taught me so much about how to break the old rules and how to expand success into all areas of life. Thanks to every one of you for being an inspiration for this book. The trust, courage, and wisdom you have brought to our sessions continue to flow out into the world.

I am deeply grateful for the three ladies and one goofy guy I get to live with. Thank you to my wife, Kathy, for holding such an amazing vision for me. Your belief and respect inspire me to climb higher and higher. You're an amazing mom and a fantastic wife! Thank you for bringing me continuous warmth, peace, and love. Karina, thank you for being such an incredible big sister for Krista and for simply being you. You radiate love. Krista, my little "clone": Thank you for making me laugh so often and for constantly bringing out the two-year-old that lives within me. And thank you to my goofy dog, Zen, for getting my butt out of the office for our daily "Zen Walk." You're a great walking partner, and you're always ready whenever I am.

And finally, to you, for reading this book. Even though we may not have met (yet), we are making a connection. Thank you!

I dedicate this book to my wife, Kathy,

whose love and belief inspires me beyond imagination.

Thank you for being my partner in so many ways.

Contents

RICH FETTKE

Part V: Make FEAR Your Friend

Part VI: Stay in the Zone

Part VII: Enjoy the High!

Foreword

The great football coach Vince Lombardi once said, "Just because you're doing something wrong—doing it more intensely isn't going to help." There's a message in those words for all of us. What he meant, of course, is that you can practice until you're exhausted, even blue in the face. You can "sweat" day after day, month after month, year after year. But if you're not doing something correctly to begin with, it's not going to make much difference. All you're doing is the wrong thing "more intensely." You're compounding—even exacerbating—the problem and reinforcing your weaknesses.

Over the years, I've learned that there's even more to it than that. I've come to believe that even if you're doing something right, doing more of it isn't necessarily going to help either. More practice, increased effort, and longer hours aren't always the answer. Effort helps, for sure, as does talent, but it can take you only so far.

That's why I was drawn to this book. While I've never thought that life was "easy," I'm certain it can be a lot easier than some of us make it out to be. Personally, I've learned that most of the time when something is "difficult," for me, it's because I'm making it more difficult than it has to be. I'm spinning my wheels or running in circles. My attention is focused in the wrong direction. In some way, I'm using my thinking against myself.

Extreme Success speaks to the heart of this matter, encouraging us to focus in the "right" direction. It helps us recognize when we are creating our own inner struggles and, in fact, getting in our own way. The book shows us how to let go of those struggles in order to pave the road toward greater success. It helps us identify and "fine tune" the "critical inch" of our efforts so that our lives become as effective and joyful as possible.

All of us have access to an inner intelligence, a source of deep wisdom. This wisdom has within it the capacity to direct our lives, answer our questions, and provide us with guidance. When we learn to trust in that wisdom, our lives become much richer, more nourishing, easier, and ultimately more successful. The way to access this wisdom, however, is not through force or effort. Instead, it becomes recognizable to us only when we are quiet, when we slow down and listen. It's almost as though we get out of our own way so that the genius inside of us has a chance to wake up. And when it does wake up, something magical begins to happen. It's as though your life is lived for you. Ideas come to you, instead of you having to search for them. Doubt is replaced with genuine confidence and an inner knowing.

Sometimes we worry too much or get ourselves all worked up. We blow little things out of proportion and end up sweating the small stuff. This problem is this: After a while, we forget that any success we do enjoy is *despite* these tendencies and certainly not *because* of them. Very often our worry, frenetic thinking, and constant rushing around are nothing more than distractions. This book will help you differentiate between that which is critical to your success and that which can be left behind.

There's often a fine line between success and failure, or winning and losing. There are also key decisions we make, attitudes we embrace, and forks in the road we travel that determine whether we are headed in the directions of our own dreams—or toward someone else's goal. Again, the key is to tap into your own inner knowing and to confidently pursue your chosen direction.

When I first met Rich Fettke and his wife, Kathy, I was immediately struck with how "at ease" both were with their lives. There was no extra effort in their way of being in the world. They were comfortable with themselves, as well as relaxed and happy. They have a loving relationship and a great deal of mutual respect for one another.

As I learned more about Rich, I realized that he was exactly what he spoke about—happy, content, successful, and doing exactly what he wanted to be doing with his life. To me, that's what Extreme Success is all about—living your dreams, above and beyond your wildest imagination. And, most important, doing so with a sense of ease and genuine joy in your heart. I am grateful that Rich Fettke was willing to share his insights with the world.

Extreme Success will point you in the direction of greater achievement with, believe it or not, less effort. There is tremendous wisdom in the pages you are about to read. I encourage you to quiet down, relax, and take the information in this book to heart. Mostly, I wish for you a life of Extreme Success and tremendous joy.

Richard Carlson
Martinez, California
September 2001

Introduction

What Is Extreme Success?

If you have achieved professional and personal success but also fear that you've accomplished everything you ever will, I want to reassure you: Extreme Success can be yours.

If you want to live out a dream, whether it's starting your own business, moving to the top of your company, traveling around the world, getting into great physical shape, or stepping beyond the apparent limits of your day-to-day life, Extreme Success can be yours.

If you have tried to follow the old success rules and find that they just don't work anymore, Extreme Success can be yours, too.

Whether you want to improve your performance, increase your income, get more out of your life—or all of the above—the strategies you need and the tools to make them happen are in your hands.

So what *is* Extreme Success? Very simply, it's a more effective, life-affirming way to succeed. At the heart of it lies the simple (yet uncommon) realization that everything can be easier. And a whole lot more fun.

Wait just a minute, you might say, this goes against everything I've read and been told.

You bet.

What about all those motivational books that told me to push hard and struggle? you might ask.

Forget about them.

I want you to break the old rules. Most people believe that they must pay a price to attain what they want, and often that price is poor health, not having enough time to enjoy life, and strained relationships with family and friends.

The old rules preached that success involved lots of homework and planning. You were directed to prepare for and then forge into the battle. Instructed to ignore your fears, overcome your weaknesses, and strain over obstacles, you may have bought into the belief that to be a success you had to fight and struggle. You were told that long—make that very long—hours of hard work were the only path to victory. You were told that achieving success wasn't about having a good life, it was about going to war! Well, not anymore.

Overpreparing and overorganizing—and, yes, even working too hard—can backfire. Struggle can actually *prevent* you from achieving the success you want. Because what you are really struggling against is *yourself.*

A counterintuitive idea? Of course. But a necessary one, because the old paradigms just don't work anymore. I've read dozens of books, attended endless seminars, and listened to hundreds of hours of audio programs. Most of them are based on a business model for success that was used fifty years ago. Today the message hasn't been changed, it's only been reformatted. Let's face it, an old typewriter with a new cartridge is still an old typewriter.

That's why I'm offering you revolutionary ideas for our revolutionary times. Technological advances keep changing the way you communicate and live. Every moment opportunities spring out of thin air. You function in a business world where the luxury of taking time to make decisions is as dated as an IBM Selectric.

But getting caught up in the wild pace of change and trying to handle it by frantically working harder and faster is like trying to swim upstream. You're only going to wear yourself out. You're not a salmon. And remember: After the salmon finishes its upstream swim, it spawns *and dies.*

The new world of business demands a new way of succeeding in it. That's what Extreme Success is all about. It will show you how to break free of the limiting perspectives of the past so that you are ready to act on the best opportunities right now and in the future. You'll succeed more and struggle less than ever before—and have a whole lot more fun in the process!

I'm going to give you something else that will change your life: a surefire approach to create your own luck.

And I'm going to show you simple and effective ways to balance your life. In my workshops I often hear variations of a common complaint. It's either "I spend so much time at work that I have to wear a name tag when I go home," or "I'm afraid to make a commitment, because I can't split myself in two. My job is so important—but so is my personal life. Or it would be—if I had one. Help!"

Guess what? *Balancing your life doesn't mean you have to compromise.* You can expand success into ALL areas of your life—and you don't have to sacrifice one element to achieve success in another. You can take your whole life to the max.

I *know* this is true. I believed that getting married and having kids would hold me back from success. Then I fell in love with a woman who already had a three-year-old daughter. I married her, but I was certain my work would suffer. Just the opposite happened. Because I wanted to spend more time with my new family, I became more focused and effective in my business. I learned a big lesson about how to work less and achieve more.

I've discovered from my own successes as well as from those of my clients that the more fun something is, the easier it is to learn and stay focused on it. Every six-year-old kid knows this intuitively. It's amazing how adults forget.

True Success Stories

I'm a certified personal coach. What's that? Well, a personal coach's approach is similar to what an athletic coach does, but with a wider focus. A personal coach takes the time to find out what winning in *life* means to you. We are specially trained to listen and observe and to help our clients succeed in all areas of life.

Coaches work with clients in all areas, including business, career, finances, health, and relationships. As a result of coaching, clients set more effective goals; devise strategies to get results; move through obstacles, difficulties, and procrastination; create more balanced and fulfilling lives, and more fully use their natural strengths. People hire me when they want more—more growth, more money, more ease, more time, more quality relationships, and more satisfaction. Bottom line: They want to get more out of life.

One of the great benefits of being a coach is the incredible education I receive from my clients. As you read, you'll find an assortment of the lessons they've taught me as well as some of my own experiences. And while we're all very different people with very different goals, it's amazing to see how the strategies that work for one client in one area can often help other people in other areas. That's one of the driving ideas behind Extreme Success, and the results are fantastic.

My clients seek my coaching to help them realize their goals, which may include career advancement, financial success, and improved personal lives. If you met these amazing people, you wouldn't be surprised at what they have accomplished—after all, their devotion to their goals is clear—but you might be surprised at how relaxed yet focused they are. There's a simple reason for their demeanor: They've found an effective, uncomplicated method to make success happen, one that doesn't rely on a sixteen-hour workday and zero personal life. I've helped them discover how this method works—and now I want to share the same strategies with you, as I did with

➤ Tamara, the owner of a large gymnastics school and rock-climbing gym, who was spending all her time and money on her businesses, to the exclusion of her family, her friends, and her *self*. By tackling her problems with new strategies, she was able to cut down her presence at work while her ventures continued to grow. She found more time to spend with her family *and* to participate in the sports she loved. Best of all, she took herself away from work—all the way to Nepal—for a real vacation.

➤ Michael, a partner in a television commercial production company, who had a $30,000 credit card debt he wanted to pay off. Michael needed help. Taking one of my suggestions, he made the crucial shift from working *in* his business to working *on* his business. In only eighteen months he raised his company's annual income from $50,000 to more than $1 million a year. And the credit card debt is gone!

➤ Christine, a financial adviser at a *Fortune* 100 investment firm for eight years, was burned out. Her income had hit a ceiling, and she had no time for herself. She wanted to "live again." I showed her how to break out of boredom and burnout. She lost more than twenty pounds, met a wonderful man, and increased her income by 200 percent over the previous three years *combined*.

Best of all, Tamara, Michael, and Christine all learned one fundamental lesson: *They stopped struggling against themselves* and were able to meet their goals—and even surpass them.

Because Extreme Success and extreme sports are linked like a parachute to a rip cord, I use my adventures as an extreme sports athlete as lessons for achievement in business and in life. Why do these lessons matter? Because in extreme sports the traditional rules are broken or just plain thrown out. We invent a new sport, a new paradigm, a new way of doing things—one that's a lot more exciting. In extreme sports, the decision about whether a challenge will be a struggle or a joy can be made before a hand is placed on a cliff or a bungee cord is tied around the ankles. The same principle applies in your professional—and personal—life.

But please don't think that you must scale a cliff or dive off a bridge to qualify as an Extreme Achiever. You don't. Extreme sports are not a prerequisite for success. Applying the *principles* involved in successfully performing the sport is what counts—and they work just as well on the Street as they do on the rock or in the air.

Ultimately, you're going to feel the astonishing exhilaration that comes from attaining what you really want—as you revel in your ability to build on past accomplishments.

TAKING YOUR SUCCESS TO THE EXTREME: SEVEN WAYS
TO MAKE IT HAPPEN

In seven quick-reading sections, I'm going to give you the tools you need to achieve Extreme Success. They are:

➤ *Create opportunity and make your own luck.* You'll learn how to be in the right place at the right time. It's not just about luck; it's about being prepared and willing to take the risk when an opportunity arises. I'll reveal the intersection where strategy meets opportunity, and take you to the place where you *can* create your own "luck."

➤ *Learn to use your strengths—and forget about those self-limiting weaknesses.* They are merely underdeveloped qualities. The key is to redirect past successes and strengths into your underdeveloped areas. That way, when opportunities arise, you will be better prepared to take action. By learning how to turn perceived "weaknesses" into strengths, pushing limits without struggle can become easy. I'll show you how it's done.

➤ *Finding the right partners and get the help you need.* There's no such thing as a self-made success: Everyone needs partners for support and creative give-and-take. In today's world, you can't compete if you can't collaborate. There are extremely effective ways to use partnerships and alliances. We'll look at what they are and how to form them.

➤ *Focus your attention on intention.* Many people allow their attention to be drawn away in lots of different ways. Encompassing everything from disorganized offices to listening to all those inner voices about what won't work, lack of attention on your goal wastes a lot of time and energy. I'll explain how your intention can reap huge rewards.

➤ *Take risks and overcome the fear factor.* This is where my four-step process to manage your fears comes into play. You'll be able to clarify what to do, when to do it, and how to avoid the pitfall of overpreparation.

➤ *Maintain the momentum you gain.* You're going to learn how to get to and stay in the "Zone" of high effectiveness. You'll experience increased confidence, heightened awareness, total concentration, and near-effortless momentum. You will learn how to keep your attention on what you truly want and how to improve your focus. I'll also help you find a challenge-ability balance so you don't become overwhelmed, frustrated, or ineffective.

➤ *Face the next challenge.* We'll look at how to widen the path of your success. This will allow you to face future challenges and opportunities with greater enjoyment, effectiveness, and ease.

Extreme Success Is in Your Future

So, are you ready to reach higher levels of success with greater joy and ease?

Are you ready to push your limits and build on what you've already accomplished?

Does the idea of using an innovative approach to reaching your highest goals—without struggling or sacrificing your life—appeal to you?

If so, then you're ready to take the leap to Extreme Success!

PART 1

Stop Struggling

1

Success Without Struggle

There are only two times I feel stress: day and night.

—Anonymous

I was ready to push my limits, to succeed at something I had never done before. That meant boarding the waiting airplane and pushing myself through a cargo door while cruising at 90 miles per hour at 14,000 feet.

I stood at this brink for one reason: I wanted to break through the unfounded terror I harbored about doing a solo jump out of an airplane. It wasn't as if I hadn't tried other boundary-breaking excursions. After all, I did bungee jump off the Golden Gate Bridge and rock climb sheer cliffs. But this was different. I really wanted to challenge myself, based on what I knew I could do—but the idea sent bolts of stark terror through me.

As I stood there, struggling with my fear, my skydiving instructor sauntered over. "Hi, I'm Billy," he drawled, offering his hand. About forty, with a three-day growth of beard, he wore a T-shirt that said SKYDIVERS: GOOD TO THE LAST DROP.

When Billy asked me if I was scared, I tried to be cool. "No. I'm not really that scared," I said with a shaky voice.

Then I let out a nervous giggle. I think Billy saw right through my act and knew how terrified I really was. Undeterred, he went over the safety instructions carefully as we put on our parachutes.

Billy and I joined a group of skydivers as we walked toward the plane. I boarded first, which meant I'd be the last one to jump. This seemed like a great plan while I was on the ground. Unfortunately, I realized that it just gave me more time to imagine what it would be like to plummet toward the earth like a meteor if the parachute didn't open.

As I pondered my fate, the other skydivers crowded into the plane. We sat on the floor in two long rows going from front to back, packed like eggs in a carton. All I could think about was what happened to Humpty Dumpty.

The higher we climbed, the faster my heart beat.

Finally, it was my turn to jump. "Remember," Billy yelled at me over the howling wind, "if you ever start to panic or struggle, just stop, be aware, and resume control." Nodding, I took a deep breath and then shouted out the protocol: "Ready . . . set . . . go!" Billy and I jumped out of the plane and into one of the most life-changing events of my life.

Billy stayed with me until we reached five thousand feet. Then he soared away so that we would have enough room to open our parachutes. As soon as I was on my own I heard that familiar nagging voice of fear that tortured me. "What are you doing out here alone?" the voice taunted me. "You're going to screw up. *You're going to die!*"

All of a sudden I lost focus and stopped arching my body the way I had been instructed. My body flipped, and I started to tumble over and over as I frantically grabbed for the rip cord. But the harder I tried, the more I missed it—and the closer I fell to the quickly approaching ground.

Then I remembered Billy's words: *Stop. Be aware. Resume*

control. In that moment I stopped struggling. I corrected my position, found the rip cord, and pulled it. *Phoomph!* A huge multicolored canopy mushroomed above me as I floated gently to earth.

I yelled in triumph as I touched down. I realized that I had overcome my fears and done something I had always dreamed about doing. Not only had I overcome my fear—I had done it twice. Once before I jumped and once after. I achieved what I came to refer to as Extreme Success, that is, using powerful strategies to dramatically expand my success into new areas. At the same time, I overcame the nearly overpowering sense of struggle that almost prevented me from fulfilling my goal. The rush I then experienced was fantastic. I felt adrenaline pumping through my body and I felt totally *alive!* I was energized and invigorated. It was an incredible feeling!

I learned an awesome lesson that day. **I discovered that struggle doesn't make success happen. In fact, struggle can *prevent* success from happening.**

This is the basis of the energizing philosophy I've adapted for my life—and the heart of my business. I've learned how to neutralize struggle, redirect fear, and stay focused so that it is possible to achieve greater success. Like me, my clients have learned how to do this. And now so can you.

Struggle: The Syndrome That Keeps On Giving

"C'mon Rich! The harder you work the better you'll be!" This belief was drummed into my head about fifteen years ago, when I was a competitive bodybuilder.

Every night at eleven o'clock, after a day working my full-time job and taking evening college classes, I would go to the gym. In the nearly deserted space I'd strain to lift weights for one more repetition while my workout partner would scream commands like, "No pain, no gain!" in my face like a drill sergeant.

Now, in bodybuilding, that may be true. It *is* important to put lots of stress on muscles to make them grow. The other lessons I learned, like discipline, focus, and visualizing my goals, also helped me to become more successful in other areas of my life. However, I took on the philosophy that the more I struggled and worked really, really hard, the more successful I would be. My problem was that I got in the habit of applying that philosophy to my *entire* life.

I also formed the skewed belief that struggle is noble. I thought that the harder I worked, the better a person I would be. Like millions of others, I bought into this counterproductive point of view. As a coach, I've heard it so many times I've coined a term for it: the Struggle Syndrome. Nobody I know embodies it better than my friend Chuck.

Chuck, Amuck

No one could ever deny that Chuck works hard. Actually, he'd be the first to agree. He delights in telling people how busy he is, how overworked, how he has no time to live because he is so overloaded. Chuck makes these statements with pride, as if he deserves multiple pats on the back for all the struggle he is putting himself through.

And struggle it certainly is. His office looks like it was arranged by a tornado. Sticky notes cover the computer screen, and to-do memos are taped all over the desk lamp. Piles teeter upon piles. Just trying to get from his office door to his desk is an extreme sport in itself.

Every January for the past several years Chuck has told

me, "This is the year I stop chasing my tail. I'm going to be organized and more effective." (As of this writing, it hasn't happened yet.)

Chuck's behavior is anything but unusual. The belief that struggle is an inseparable partner of success is deeply ingrained in our society; it's something I hear from just about all my clients. When I ask them why they feel this way, they usually say, "My parents always told me that if I wanted to make it big I had to work hard. And every time a colleague succeeds, you always hear someone say, 'Wow, he really worked hard for that. He deserves the recognition he's getting.'" They quote from self-help books they've read and seminars they've attended, all of which stress the effort of success and involve breaking through obstacles and making great personal sacrifices on the road to achievement. They believe that the reward for a job well done is more work. Is it any surprise that they usually feel overwhelmed and/or burned out?

Ultimately, they equate success with pain and end up filtering their work—and their lives—through the assumption that struggle is inevitable. The result is that other options don't get any consideration. When this happens it's time to remove the struggle filter and look at life through a wide-angle lens that reveals a much bigger picture with many more choices.

So when my clients start to brag about how busy they are, I shock them by saying, "Oh, I'm sorry to hear that. How would you like your worklife to be?"

This opposing view begins to shift people from their rigid mind-set and helps them approach success in a different way. Then I tell them what I'm telling you: It took a leap out of an airplane for me to understand that struggle isn't only not noble—it can be life-threatening!

I sum up my strategy like this:
If you seek struggle, you will find it.
If you seek ease, you will find it.

I believe in trusting that things are going to go *well*. And while I know it's crucial to prepare for the worst, I also expect the best. I realize this is an unconventional outlook, but I know how important it is to be open to the idea that success can happen with joy and ease, not struggle and frustration.

This doesn't mean that I don't believe in challenge. There's nothing I embrace more than the thought of achieving something new that's going to require real effort. What I don't believe is that effort automatically links with struggle, which further links to negativity. *All struggle produces is a situation where enjoyment is sucked out of what you're doing—even if the outcome is successful.*

No Pain, All Gain

You don't have to leap out of an airplane and lose control to feel the impact of the Struggle Syndrome. My coaching clients report lots of various Struggle Syndrome symptoms. Having headaches or a tight neck, snapping at coworkers, forgetting appointments, losing things—these are all struggle signs.

I know when my own struggle bug starts to bite. I clench my jaw, jump from project to project, and build mountains of papers on my desk. Not surprisingly, I become distracted and even frantic. Now, however, when the symptoms first kick in, I can stop them quickly by asking myself, How can I do this with greater ease? Occasionally I do all of the following actions, sometimes just one or two.

1. I shift my mind-set from "I have to do this" to "I'm choosing to do this."
2. I stand up and take a couple of deep breaths.
3. I break what I'm doing into small "chunks."
4. I go for a walk.
5. I clean up my work space.
6. I choose only one project to focus on and "hide" all the others.
7. I work on something else and come back to the project when I'm in a better mood and willing to focus on it again.
8. I ask for help.

These choices help me to step back, become more alert, and look for a more effective way to accomplish what I'm working on. Once the Struggle Syndrome kicks in I stop, become aware, and resume control.

Isn't it time you gave yourself the permission to succeed with ease, too? It's a much more effective and joyful way to live and work.

Meet my client Lisa, in her mid-thirties, who learned how to succeed with ease. Lisa's personal fitness trainer, whom she saw whenever she was in the San Francisco area for her work, referred her to me.

Before I start to coach, I always send a series of questionnaires to the new client to fill out before our initial meeting. I sent these forms to Lisa, who had just begun a job as a salesperson for a medical supply company in the Midwest.

When asked what main areas she wanted to focus on, Lisa wrote:

1. *Increase my sales.* I want to be the #1 salesperson in my company. I'm willing to do whatever it takes to achieve this goal!

2. *Stop procrastinating!* I have so many things I want to do, but I never have the time or energy to complete them. I have so much to do, but I can't keep up with everything. Every time I turn around, there's something else I need to do.

At our first meeting I asked Lisa, "What's the biggest obstacle that might get in your way of becoming the number-one salesperson at your company?"

Lisa said, "Look at the second thing I want to focus on: procrastination! I want to move forward, but it feels like I have too many things just to catch up on. I feel like I'm on overload and about to go into overwhelm."

As a "homework" assignment, I asked Lisa to make a list of all those things that she "had to catch up on." She agreed.

The following week she brought the list. I began our session by saying, "Okay, let's see what you can eliminate or delegate." Lisa was adamant: "I can't! All those things are my responsibility. Anyway, if I try to get someone else to do them they'll probably do them wrong and then I'll have to fix their mistakes. That will take longer than just doing it myself."

"How do you know that they will do them wrong?" I asked.

"I just know it."

But when I said, "Please just trust me on this one. Let's go through the list, okay?" Lisa agreed.

As we began, Lisa was very uncomfortable with the idea of letting go of total control. It was obvious that she assumed that reaching her goal was going to be brutal, because even before the first coaching session, Lisa had set up her own struggling strategies.

She told me about how she had considered working twelve-hour days to "catch up." Of course, that entailed giving up a few things, like not working out at her gym for a few months. Lisa assumed that struggle, in order to achieve her sales goal, was inevitable.

"Lisa," I told her, "as long as you keep telling yourself that what you want to accomplish is going to be hard, it will be. Let's look at a different perspective. What would it be like if you had space in your schedule to focus on what really matters for great sales?"

Lisa didn't say anything for a moment. Then she replied, "Peaceful."

"Great! It *can* be that way if you tell yourself it *will* be that way. Are you willing to take on that perspective? I know it's an unconventional way of approaching a goal, but I believe it's really important to be open to it. It's the best way—the only way—to bring you success with joy and ease, not struggle and frustration. Look at it this way: If your desire is to ski, why hike up the mountain and wear yourself out when you can take the chairlift?"

Lisa nodded. "I'm willing to try," she said.

Line by line we began to go through her list again. This time, Lisa was much more willing to cross off the not truly vital to-do's. She was also much more willing to take what she called the "risk" of delegating many of the remaining tasks from her list.

From that point on, she began looking for the most effective and enjoyable ways to reach her goal. She hired an assistant to whom she delegated many of her tasks. At the same time, Lisa continued with her workout program and kept her commitment to work no more than nine hours per day.

Throughout this book we'll follow Lisa's story, along with those of several of my other coaching clients. You'll see what happens with Lisa's stress, how she does with her goals, and what happens when she breaks free of the Struggle Syndrome.

Keepers: Thoughts to Remember

➤ Struggle doesn't make success happen. In fact, struggle can *prevent* success from happening.

➤ If you seek struggle, you will find it. If you seek ease, you will find it.

➤ Learn to stop, be aware, and resume control.

➤ Notice how you start falling into the Struggle Syndrome. Write down what red flags start flying.

➤ Decide what you will do when you notice that you're struggling or losing control.

➤ Write a personal affirmation to help bring you back to grounded effectiveness as you stop, become aware, and resume control.

Action Idea #1: Learn to Work with Ease

1. Think about your past week. Write down one way that you made the process of going for your goals harder and less effective.

2. Now write down how you could have made the process more effective and enjoyable.

3. On the same day each week go through this ritual. Week by week you will develop a stronger ability to avoid the Struggle Syndrome. You'll find that you will become more effective (and happier) as time goes on. If you want to raise your level of awareness even further, begin this ritual by rating how the week was for you on a scale of 1 to 10. (With 10 being very effective, joyful, and struggle-free.)

2

X Marks the Spot

Opportunity doesn't knock. You knock and opportunity answers.

—Anonymous

During the Great Blizzard of 1978, when Massachusetts schools were closed for a whole week, my little brother, Steve, and I reaped the rewards of record-breaking snowfalls.

As soon as there was a letup in the weather, Steve and I headed out looking for adventure. Arriving at Thorpe Elementary School, we couldn't believe our eyes. It was as if Mount Everest had just dropped out of the sky and landed in the schoolyard. Snowbanks reached the school's roof, three stories up.

All that snow was irresistible. We climbed up and up until we made it onto the roof, which overlooked the parking lot. Below us lay an impressive thirty-five- to forty-foot drop to ground level.

Based partly on the fact that I liked to jump and partly because the opportunity presented itself, I made the kind of quick decision a thirteen-year-old boy is apt to make.

"I'm gonna jump," I yelled.

Steve watched in disbelief as I took a running start, leapt into the air, let out a big "yahooooo," and landed in the soft snowbank below. I dug my way out of the silent darkness and climbed back up to coerce my nine-year-old brother to jump. "Now it's your turn," I told him, breathless with excitement. "No way!" he said, turning a shade paler than the snow. But seeing my flushed face and the crazy gleam in my eyes, there was no way he was going to let me call him a coward.

Steve backed up slowly as he steeled himself to rush the edge. Crying and running, he leapt off the roof and disappeared into the snowbank. I peered over the edge and listened. My first thought was, Oh my God! Mom's gonna kill me. Then Steve emerged, ecstatic—once he realized he hadn't broken both his legs.

On that day, my brother and I discovered the intersection where strategy meets opportunity. And though I didn't know it then, I had taken my first leap toward Extreme Success.

You Want Me to Take a Giant Leap Where?

Years later, when Steve was attending college in California, he hooked up with a roommate who had the bungee bug. Steve videotaped a few of their jumps and sent them to me. Watching, I felt like I was on the other end of the cord. I headed out west.

After my first jump of 230 feet, Steve and I used topographical maps to locate the highest, most remote bridges to practice our moves. Then one of Steve's friends, a cameraman at a local TV station, said, "Hey, I'd love to do some shots of you guys." He sent the footage to ESPN. Their response was to schedule the first *North American Bungee Jump-*

Off Competition. Fifteen jumpers plunged off a 170-foot bridge over the rapids of the Feather River. My little brother, the kid who had cried all the way to the edge of the Thorpe School roof, took first place. I followed up in third.

Meanwhile, ESPN execs were talking about a totally new sporting event called the X Games. Bungee jumping made the cut, and Steve and I received a letter inviting us to submit an X Games application. Not only did they want a signed release that let them off the hook if we killed our crazy selves; they also wanted a video. We had to prove that we could do three front flips off the platform with a front flip on the rebound along with three *back* flips off the platform and a back flip on the way back up.

Opportunity Meets Strategy

Wild, huh? Even better, we had less than one week. The question was, Do we do this or bag it? We could have said, "Hey, we just don't have time to go out, find a bridge that we could jump without getting arrested, practice these moves, and *then* make a video." Or we could have listened to our inner voices telling us, "Forget it, man! You'll never get chosen to compete anyway. Face it—you're just a coupla yahoos out for thrills!" But, hey—not a chance! We knew how to jump and a terrific opportunity had presented itself. We were up for doing whatever it took to succeed.

We found an old, secluded bridge in a canyon near Lake Tahoe and went there at night to practice, using our

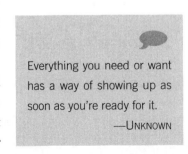

Everything you need or want has a way of showing up as soon as you're ready for it.

—UNKNOWN

truck lights for illumination. Sure we were scared, but we were psyched enough to keep jumping before the car battery died. We sent the tape to ESPN, and within a week Steve got the call. *We were going to the games!*

People said we were lucky. We were—but I didn't realize at that moment how our luck came to us.

Taking the Leap

So there I was in Rhode Island, riding a construction elevator to the jump tower, which was a huge crane used on skyscraper construction sites. Looming 160 feet above a downtown Providence park, the tower was situated above a large reflecting pool containing only two feet of water. *This* was the target.

Finally I reached the X Games staff, who then prepped me. Once the cord was tightly wound and knotted around my ankles, I hopped the final distance to the edge of the giant boom—like walking the plank off the Empire State Building, I thought—gripped the edge with my toes and looked down.

The target resembled a tiny plastic pool I had splashed in as a kid. Thousands of people watched from their comfy blankets and lawn chairs. I took a big breath, let out a yell, cranked four front flips off the platform, and then nailed a back flip on the rebound. It was a blast!

Even though Steve and I lost out to a Canadian who outmaneuvered everyone else, I knew I had hit upon something big (obviously not that reflecting pool).

I realized what we had done to get where we were. When that great opportunity presented itself, we were not only prepared, we were also willing to take action. And while people said we were lucky, I realized something better.

I saw how X marks the spot where luck is created.

Follow the X to Extreme Success

Imagine a big X. The left leg of the X represents strategy. The right leg represents opportunity. *The point of intersection is the place where extreme success happens—if you take action.*

If you strategize but overprepare and overplan, you can pass right through the intersection. On the other hand, if you don't have a strategy you'll never even *reach* the intersection.

When you reach that intersection, then you are ready to seize the opportunity that awaits you. Bill Gates, for instance, knew when X marked his spot.

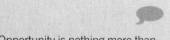

> Opportunity is nothing more than— vapor. It is a condition, or an atmosphere that is created and made available. It's up to you to make it a reality. Nothing—and that means nothing—happens in your life until you make something happen.
>
> —GARY RYAN BLAIR,
> *MIND MUNCHIES*

Bill Gates: One "Lucky" Guy

In the early 1980s IBM was looking for an operating system to power its newly designed personal computers. First they approached Digital Research, a company founded by Gary Kildall in 1974. But Kildall didn't foresee the high-tech revolution in personal computers. He didn't like what IBM was offering and held on to his system. He believed a lot more money was waiting down the road.

Meanwhile, Bill Gates's mother, who just happened to sit on the same charity board as an IBM exec, referred Big Blue to Gates. Unlike Kildall, Gates was ready and willing to accept IBM's offer. Was Kildall just plain unlucky? Or was Gates one very lucky guy? Both were confronted with the same opportunity, but only one person saw it and was prepared to act on it.

Have you ever failed to step back and take a good look at the "intersections" in your life? (Of course you have; otherwise you wouldn't be here with me.)

What stopped you from taking advantage of a great opportunity when it stared you in the face?

Maybe the intense need to know the outcome of a situation held you back. Perhaps it was the lack of a perfect plan or a guarantee of success. Maybe it was more basic. Fear may have stopped you.

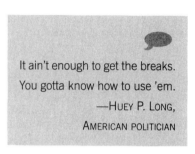

It ain't enough to get the breaks. You gotta know how to use 'em.

—HUEY P. LONG,
AMERICAN POLITICIAN

Would luck have made a difference?

Where Is Your Luck?

Put a check next to the one sentence that really describes your attitude toward luck.

1. ＿＿＿Luck is just a matter of chance. No one can "create" it.

2. ＿＿＿Some people just know how to make luck. I'm not one of them.

3. ＿＿＿I could create more luck in my life. I just haven't done much about it.

4. ＿＿＿I am actively preparing myself for luck *if* it comes my way.

5. _____ I am actively preparing myself for luck *when* it comes my way.

6. _____ I've created luck in the past and I'm actively preparing for more.

7. _____ I am a lucky person. I don't even prepare myself and I attract luck with ease.

Scoring: The statements above are arranged from a low to a high belief about the ability to create luck. If you checked:

1 or 2: Your beliefs might be pushing you to feel like a "victim." You might feel that there is no chance that you can achieve success unless fate has it planned that way. If you don't start working on your belief about the role that you can play in creating luck, you probably won't either see it or trust it when it shows up.

3 or 4: You can see that being lucky may depend a lot on you. Continue to prepare yourself and reinforce the belief that opportunities are coming. Keep seeking them. When the opportunities do arrive, you will be better prepared to notice them as well as act on and benefit from them.

5 or 6: You obviously believe in a "luck attraction" attitude. You realize that you can prepare for and be aware of opportunities that can help you generate even more luck. Keep that great attitude and you'll be on the fast track to Extreme Success.

7: Be careful! Your optimistic attitude about luck is attractive, but you may be setting yourself up for future failure or missed

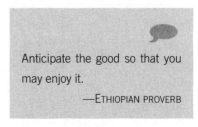

Anticipate the good so that you may enjoy it.
—ETHIOPIAN PROVERB

opportunities. Maintain your positive belief and prepare yourself for the opportunities that could help you reach your goals. This way your great luck will continue!

"Do Ya Feel Lucky . . . Well, Do Ya?"

I've had clients who went on and on about how unlucky they were. They didn't believe that luck would come their way.

I've also had other clients who believed they were very lucky. Their attitude was what I'll call "luck attraction." Like a self-fulfilling prophecy, they invented a lucky personality by saying to themselves, "Yes, opportunities *are* coming to me, and I accept them and appreciate and notice them." Their luck was *intentional*.

Intentional luck happens when strategy meets an opportunity and action takes place. What shuffles some people into the unlucky deck is their inability to use opportunities. Not only are they not taking advantage of them, they completely fail to see them! Why? *Because they're not intentionally looking.* They're too busy struggling with their to-do list or feeling unprepared to notice. It's as if they're in a mine they're told is full of diamonds, but because they haven't brought a pick, they don't bother looking for them.

I know luck can be produced. Here's how Bud, a client of mine, learned how to do it.

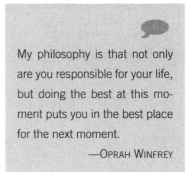

My philosophy is that not only are you responsible for your life, but doing the best at this moment puts you in the best place for the next moment.

—OPRAH WINFREY

Hey Bud, What's Your Story?

My client, Bud, thirty-nine, was a professional storyteller who hit a snag. While he booked a decent number of engagements to entertain at corporate banquets, schools, and private parties, his fee was mediocre. Disorganized, he found himself bogged down in his office. Chronic lower back pain plagued him, and since he was barely making ends meet, his stress level was reaching critical mass.

When Bud and I began working together, one of the things I asked him was, "How would you rate your office satisfaction level, from one to ten?" He gave it a lackluster 3. When I asked him where he would like it to be, he said he would settle for a comfortable 8.

We set his goal at that number, and each week he'd take some kind of action to clean up and organize. Between our weekly check-ins and my support, he climbed from a 3.5 to a 4 and finally to 8.

Because sitting at his computer hurt his back, I challenged him to work out three times a week to strengthen his stomach muscles and ease the stress on his lower back. Starting to feel better, he could work for longer periods without discomfort.

Bud and I then began working on specific strategies to raise his income. Since he was able to put in more writing and creative time in the office, he turned his focus to his marketing materials, which included a biography listing his accomplishments.

Then it happened. Bud got a call from a friend who worked for one of the world's top food distributors. His corporation wanted to tell how it developed its values and became such a huge success. They planned to use this information to inspire and educate new managers and salespeople. Since the friend knew Bud to be the consummate storyteller, he suggested, "Why don't you call them up?"

He did.

Bud wanted to be completely prepared for his meeting with the company execs. I asked him what top three points he wanted to make. First, he intended to draw out the story *from* them, rather than tell the story *for* them. Second, he wanted them to know that he wasn't just a "suit." He would wear his special vest, the one that made him *feel* like a storyteller, and then tell them stories. Third, he wanted to have fun.

The day of the big meeting, Bud stuck to his three points, and the execs knew they had a winner. They said they were very interested in having Bud go around the country to talk with their company's movers and shakers to draw out their unique stories. Then they threw Bud a curve: "Draw up a proposal for us and let us know how much this is going to cost."

Knowing what corporations pay for speakers and consultants, I knew the initial price Bud planned to quote was way too low. The execs would think his work would not be high quality. I knew that if he charged *three times* what he thought he should, it would be more in sync with the corporate world. I also knew that if I told Bud that, he would probably want to negotiate down lower. So I used a different tactic.

"You're going to have to raise your rates about five hundred percent of what you're telling me," I said to him on the phone. Suddenly, I heard him choking on his drink.

"I can't do that," he sputtered. "They won't want to hire me!"

We settled on 300 percent, and when he quoted the price, the execs didn't flinch. He got the job and collected stories that were eventually a basis for the company's "autobiography" and employee training program.

Bud built his own intentional luck. Though he didn't realize it at the outset, Bud followed a strategy to prepare himself for just this kind of opportunity. He cleaned up his office and organized new space in his life. He took care of his back, preparing himself for the work that lay ahead. He set up our partnership, which challenged him to clarify what he wanted in his future. All these preparations allowed him to recognize—and go for—a life-changing opportunity when it arose. Bud's being "at the right place at the right time" was not an accident.

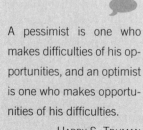

A pessimist is one who makes difficulties of his opportunities, and an optimist is one who makes opportunities of his difficulties.

—HARRY S. TRUMAN

It was intentional luck. He created his own Extreme Success!

Moving Forward

As you move through this book, you will better understand how to get to the X intersection. You'll learn new ways to strategize and prepare yourself to create intentional luck. You will also be better able to recognize when you've reached the intersection. And you will have new ways to overcome the resistance and fear that often show up when it's time to take action. With this knowledge you will achieve more of what you want with less effort. Don't be surprised when people start calling *you* lucky.

Keepers: Thoughts to Remember

➤ Do things to ready yourself and always be looking for the intersections where strategy meets opportunity.

➤ Gaining clarity on what you want for your desired outcomes will help you know what to look for.

➤ Keep telling yourself that you *are* lucky. The more your mind hears this the more it will believe it.

➤ Think about where you have produced luck in your past and how that happened. There are indicators to help you now and in the future.

➤ Observe other people who you believe to be lucky and note what they did to get that way.

➤ Creating luck often means preparing yourself to take a risk and learning to deal with your fears.

➤ Developing partnerships and alliances with others can help you improve your chances.

Action Idea #2: Take Just One Step

Identify one step, however small, that you have been putting off that might help you prepare for a future opportunity. This week take action. Tell your coach or a friend what you will do and ask him or her to hold you accountable to following through. Make a commitment to check in next week to say that you've taken action. You'll discover what a powerful impact this simple act can have on your personal and professional effectiveness as well as your peace of mind.

3

Balance Your Extremes

It's a funny thing about life—if you refuse to accept anything but the very best you will often get it.

—W. Somerset Maugham

"YOLO! You only live once!"

This is the way Gerald, one of my best friends, answers his phone. An international karate champion who is a member of the U.S. Kenpo Karate Team, he has won matches in Europe and in the States. The owner of a successful martial arts center, he is also a licensed financial adviser.

"G" is a master at balancing. Consciously, he shifts his attention and focus to various areas of his life at different times. *Consciously* is the key word here. He decides how, and for how long, he will set his focus on a certain area of his life. He also determines when he is going to shift that focus.

Gerald lives by a certain standard: No matter what he does, he *balances extremes.*

This means attaining a tremendous level of satisfaction and fulfillment in all areas of his life. Gerald understands that balance is not about compromise. It's about choice. Settle for less? Forget about it. Settle for more is more like it.

Here's G's step-by-step strategy as he prepares for a competition:

1. Knowing the date of his next meet far in advance, he plans out the coming fourteen weeks. Creating a plan that focuses his thoughts and energy on achieving his goal, he decides how much he wants to weigh and how he wants to fight. His intended outcome is always the same: first place.

2. He puts systems in place for his day-to-day living. Work schedules are adjusted and a training schedule is laid out. He creates a strict nutritional program, which includes four to five small meals a day, and he measures his caloric, carbohydrate, protein, and fat intake. As part of his training he places a few beers in his fridge so that every time he opens the door they stare him in the face. Since he makes a commitment not to drink any alcohol during his training period, this helps him confirm how mentally strong he really is.

3. He discusses his plan with his fiancée and other important people in his life, including the people at his martial arts center. Instructors, training partners, and students help support him and often benefit from the inspiration and the focus that is placed on the big goal.

4. Every evening he visualizes the entire day of his fight. He sees himself getting up in the morning with confidence and power and finishing the match by pumping his arms in the air to celebrate his victory.

After the competition, G transfers his focus over to fun, relaxation, and self-care. He takes a week off from any type of physical training, drinks those beers, and gives himself permission to gain five to seven pounds because it's all part of the plan. One hundred percent results, zero percent guilt.

After his relaxation phase, G swings his focus to his next major goal. This might be increasing his income, nurturing his relationship, deepening his spirituality, or arranging a major fund-raiser for charity.

Instead of a moderate focus and a modest effort, G uses intense focus and puts an incredible effort into everything he does. Whatever big outcome he wants to achieve, he doesn't just tap on its surface: He kicks his way through. G has found that this strategy and process bring him exceptional results in other areas of his life as well. His businesses are thriving; he's in great shape; he enjoys a wonderful relationship with his fiancée, and he always has a big grin on his face. How could he not? He achieves success without struggle.

From There to Here, From Here to There

If you take a look at what G does to achieve his goals, there is one constant: He *moves;* he is always *balancing* his life. He knows it's impossible to balance while standing still.

So it's time to throw out that old standard of equilibrium, those two dusty perfectly aligned scales. You know why? Because they are static, and they aren't going anywhere.

Life balance requires constant motion in order to give all the factors that make life worth living equal weight. That means readjusting yourself when you concentrate all your energy on acquiring possessions but lack a friend to ski with. It requires correcting an all-out assault on your work with no time to let off steam. It might mean putting extra focus on growing your business if most of your attention is on planning your vacation. It demands fine-tuning your life so that you make the best music you can. After all, if you aren't the conductor who balances the instruments of your life, who is?

Balancing extremes means creating incredible success in all areas of your life, not just one. Balance is a skill that can be developed. If you want to get the most out of life, it's a skill you need—and deserve—to master.

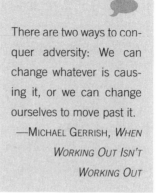

There are two ways to conquer adversity: We can change whatever is causing it, or we can change ourselves to move past it.
—MICHAEL GERRISH, WHEN WORKING OUT ISN'T WORKING OUT

Christine's Unbalancing Act

At thirty-three, Christine, a financial adviser who had been working at the same investment firm for over eight years, couldn't find any balance in her life. "It's pretty ironic," she told me at our first meeting, "I'm supposed to create balance in other people's lives by giving them sound money advice. But in my own life it's nonexistent. My income has flattened out. Even worse, I feel like I'm on a seesaw, sitting on the ground, and no one is on the other end. I used to wake up and look forward to my day. Now the gravitational pull of my bed is so strong I want to stay there with the covers pulled over my head. I have no energy, no will to take better care of myself. I've gained over twenty-five pounds in the last year, and I hate the way I look. But I feel helpless to do anything about it. I used to have a handle on my life—but it broke. Every day I ask myself, Where's my life?"

This confession hit my heart like a Mike Tyson punch. It drives me crazy to see a washed-out life. To help Christine break out of her boredom and burnout spiral, I needed an idea of how she felt about the different areas of her life. In order to get a "snapshot" of her current condition I asked her to fill out the Life Balance Wheel. This is a tool I use to help my clients see how satisfied they are with the different parts of their lives and how they are balancing them. (I use it, too.) I asked her to rate her satisfaction level from 10 (extremely incredible) to 1 (yuck!). A 10 earned a line at the outer edge of the wheel, while 1 deserved a line near the center. Anything between 2 and 9 would be placed in between. Here's what Christine's wheel looked like.

Christine's Life Balance Wheel
March

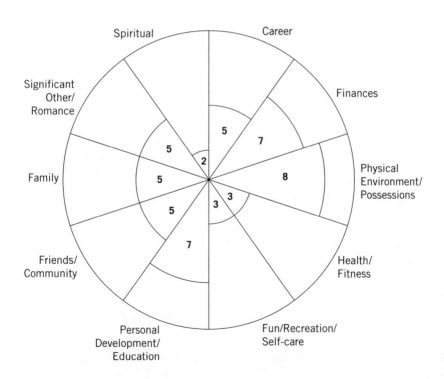

Looking at the wheel, I asked Christine, "How bumpy would the ride be if this were a wheel on your car?" She laughed, but I could detect the frustration underneath. "It would be pretty uncomfortable," she admitted. "But I don't follow. I'm working with you to increase my motivation and raise my income. Fun, self-care, romance, fitness: What do these have to do with that?"

"Stand up," I replied. "Close your eyes and lift your right foot and keep it up." As she did, Christine extended her arms like a hawk catching an updraft. "Notice what your body is doing. Feel it."

Christine muttered, "I'm about to tip over." I got closer to her and whispered, "But you're not tipping over. Notice the small corrections your body is making. When you start to lose balance, your body makes bigger adjustments."

Christine nodded.

"Notice that even when you feel like you are perfectly balanced, you are still making little adjustments to stay standing. Feel all those little muscles that are working to keep you vertical. You are *balancing*. Okay, go ahead and open your eyes. And have a seat.

"Life balance is about noticing when you are leaning too far into one part of your life and then consciously moving toward another to keep from falling. Sometimes those adjustments are small; other times they are big. Bottom line: You have to stay aware of which way you are tipping and keep moving into other areas. If you keep leaning toward only one area, you will fall on your face."

Christine sat up with renewed interest. "So you're saying that if I don't start dating that I'm going to topple over?"

"Based on the satisfaction rating of five, yes you will. I've seen this many, many times. Once you begin to improve your satisfaction in the areas of your life that don't seem to be working for you, you'll see that all the other areas begin to work better, too. I've seen this work for too many clients not to believe it. My job is to help my clients move from thinking 'That's just the way it is' to 'What other options do I have?' awareness. And I know life balance does this."

Then Christine told me that she hadn't taken a vacation in three years and kept avoiding the dating "scene" because she felt insecure about her body.

We came up with a plan that would have a positive impact on her health and fitness, fun and self-care. She said that she wasn't ready to start dating again but that we could revisit that in the future.

Right away, Christine made a commitment to exercise and to take a one-week vacation every quarter for one year. Because she was responsible for her own business development and made her own hours, this was very doable. It also made her much more effective when she was working. She prepared herself for each vacation by getting clear on her ideal day. Here is her plan:

1. Watch no more than one hour of television per night. (She had previously been flipping channels for two to three hours a night.)

2. Prepare a healthy lunch for the next day.

3. Get to bed one hour earlier and wake up one hour earlier.

4. First thing in the morning, do a half-hour walk on her treadmill (which she had previously been using as a clothing rack).

5. Invest a half-hour every morning to plan her day.

A month later Christine had achieved some great results. She had lost seven pounds and hopped out of bed in the morning with new energy. She felt, as she put it, "like life was working again." And—no surprise to me—her income had exceeded her best month ever by nearly 10 percent! I'd say that these are some pretty good results

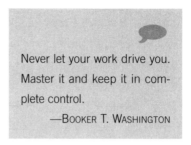

Never let your work drive you. Master it and keep it in complete control.

—Booker T. Washington

from a few small "shifts" in where she was putting her focus. It's another great example of achieving success without struggle.

How Are You Rolling Along?

It's time to fill in your own Life Balance Wheel. In each section of the wheel, draw a line that corresponds to your current level of satisfaction in that area of your life. When you've labeled and drawn a line in each section corresponding to your level of satisfaction from 1 to 10, just like Christine did, step back and look at the shape of the wheel. There it is, your current life balance.

Big reality check, isn't it?

Sometimes balancing demands getting uncomfortable and doing things differently and dealing with old issues in new ways. It's just like when I am hiking up to a cliff that I plan to climb. The closer I get, the more ominous it looks. The same is true as you get closer to taking action on a new way of living. Still, it's worth the risk. When you push your limits, you find out what you are actually capable of. Usually it is much more than you had previously believed.

A successful person is a complete person. Have you ever heard someone say something like, "I'm different at work than I am at home"? That's an indicator that he or she is not living true to who they really are. They think they have to wear different masks, such as "the pleaser" or the "tough boss" or the "loving father," to look like they have it together. The key to balance is understanding what you truly want in the different areas of your life and then taking steps to achieve them.

Balancing your wheel takes courage and honesty. Balance is not a destination that you can just get to and then stay at. It's about consistent awareness and action. Remember: *Balance is not a compromise position.* You don't have to give up on one area of your life to get more of another. The more attention you pay to all aspects of your life, the more balanced you will be.

What you value is all-important. You may want to slow down, to simplify your life, and have more space. Your co-worker may want to experience more thrills and breakthroughs. There is no right or wrong. It's up to you to identify how you desire to live your life, and then it's up to you to live it that way. No matter what you decide, you must balance your life to achieve it. Otherwise, you're just going to keep struggling.

Near the end of this chapter is a blank Life Balance Wheel. Make several copies of the wheel and then fill one out every quarter to see how you're doing. Don't look at the

Be glad of life because it gives you the chance to love and to work and to play and to look at the stars.

—HENRY VAN DYKE, EARLY TWENTIETH-CENTURY AMERICAN WRITER

previous wheels until you've filled out the new one. Then look at what you changed as you smooth the bumps.

Keepers: Thoughts to Remember

➤ Balancing extremes yields incredible success in *all* areas of your life.

➤ You create a more balanced life by *consciously* shifting your attention and focus to various areas of your life at different times. Life balance requires constant motion.

➤ Move from thinking, That's just the way it is, to asking, What other options do I have? This is a major key to achieving greater success without struggle.

➤ Sometimes balancing your life demands doing things differently and dealing with old issues in new ways.

➤ *Balance is not a compromise position.* You don't have to give up on one area of your life to get more of another. The more attention you pay to all the aspects of your life, the more balanced you will be. Otherwise, you're just going to keep struggling.

Action Idea #3: See New Possibilities

Challenge yourself to come up with at least five different ways to look at a situation or a solution to a problem that is troubling you. Pick your favorite perspective. What might your life be like if you lived this way or if you took this action? Imagine it is reality. If the possibilities look good, then come up with a plan of action and commit to it. Check in with your coach or a friend to tell them how you're doing with your plan. This will help you get unstuck and propel you into action.

Action Idea #4: Eliminate or Delegate

Identify something you are doing that you do not enjoy. How could you take that activity off of your "plate"? For instance, could you just stop doing it? Could you delegate it? Could you pay someone else to do it? Challenge yourself to take one thing off your plate this week. You will most likely notice that you can have more of what you want with greater joy and ease.

Action Idea #5: Assess Your Life Balance

This is an important step to get the most out of this book. If you haven't done it already, use the Life Balance Wheel to assess your satisfaction in the different areas of your life and how you are balancing them. We'll be coming back to your wheel in a future chapter.

Life Balance Wheel

Date:_____

Spiritual

Career

work

heart

Significant
Other/
Romance

Finances

b

EXTREME SUCCESS

Family

social

Physical
Environment/
Possessions

stuff

Friends/
Community

Health/
Fitness

body

Personal
Development/
Education

ed.

Fun/Recreation/
Self-care

self

mind
body
spirit

) self

others —

PART 2

PART 2

Get Ready to Go Big

4

The Courage for Change

"On a visit to California, a Zen master went into a coffee shop to buy a cup of tea. He handed the guy at the counter a ten-dollar bill. The employee stuck the money in the cash drawer. When the Zen master asked, 'What about my change?' The guy looked up at him and said, 'Dude, as you know, change comes from within.'"

Jim shook his head in disbelief as I told this story to him yet again. "You must be crazy!" he huffed nervously at me as we stood at the edge of a 90-foot cliff on Mount Diablo, 3,800 feet of stunning sandstone near San Francisco.

"Come on, Jim, look in my eyes. I know you can do this. It's another part of the Plan." "The Plan" was a strategic process we developed when he hired me to help him transform his body. This was another step of his "rite of passage" into Extreme Success, a process that began at sea level and took him to incredible heights.

Just six months before, when I first met Jim, he could barely lift himself out of a chair. He was turning forty, his wife was expecting a baby, and he realized that dragging himself around feeling old and unhealthy was not the way to live. It wasn't that Jim wasn't successful. In a purely financial way, he certainly was. He had nurtured his landscaping company into a million-dollar monster that fed on trucks, tractors, trailers, and a huge crew of workers. The problem was that with all the focus on growing his company, Jim's belly had expanded just as fast.

With forty pounds of excess fat weighing down his six-foot frame, Jim was in mental and physical pain. His lower back constantly plagued him, and he wore all his shirts untucked to hide his girth. He was having a classic "midline" crisis.

About this time, I had sold my health club in Massachusetts and moved to California to start a company called Bio-Focus, which provided one-on-one personal fitness training in a private studio. Jim saw an ad I had placed in a local newspaper with a headline that read, I CAN HELP YOU LOOK AND FEEL INCREDIBLE! (Yeah, yeah, looking back on it now I can't believe how corny that was. But it worked!) Jim left me a voice mail with his phone number.

I called him back and left a message on his answering machine. He didn't call back. Two days later I left another message. Same deal. A day later I tried again, but Jim never called me back. I thought, Should I just leave this guy alone? I must seem like a pain in the butt. But something inside me said, This guy called for a reason. He wants to change his life. Call him one more time. This time, when I dialed the phone, Jim answered.

He told me, "I'm fat, I'm in pain, and I don't want to end up dying early on my children. I don't know what to do." Jim related how he had tried different weight-loss programs and failed. He was fearful that if he was unsuccessful one more time he would totally give up on himself. Then I asked, "And what will happen if you don't give it one more shot?"

That hit home. Jim agreed to meet me.

After a couple hours of discussing his needs, filling out questionnaires, and doing some physical tests, Jim and I created The Plan.

He committed to:

➤ work out with weights three times per week;

➤ reduce coffee intake to two cups a day (from his previous six to eight cups);

➤ walk for at least a half hour three times a week;

➤ reduce the amount of high-fat foods he was eating by half;

➤ indulge in whatever he wanted to eat one day a week;

➤ go to a chiropractor for an assessment of his low-back pain.

Jim amazed himself and me. He made a 100 percent commitment to his plan day in and day out. Six months later he had lost thirty-six pounds, hummed with energy, and was overjoyed that his chiropractor had helped cure his back pain.

Then one morning I got a call. "Rich, I know I haven't missed a workout, but today I have to. My baby boy just arrived!" Jim was thrilled. By harnessing his inner courage, he had broken free of his past to create a new way of living.

What a gift he gave to his son. What a gift he gave to himself.

Then he told me that he wanted to go to the "next level."

"I've never felt as incredible as I'm feeling right now!" he exclaimed. "I want more!"

That's why we were perched, condor-eye level, on Mount Diablo. Now Jim was a human spider about to zip down a mountain—even if he was a bit jittery. He and I were going to rappel, which involves lowering yourself backward off a cliff using a single rope and a waist harness. I was standing right in front of him and holding on to the straps that connected his rappel rope to a couple of big oak trees at the top of the cliff.

Jim squeezed the rope so hard his knuckles were white. His body trembled, and he was breathing faster than he did during his most intense cardio workout.

"Jim, it's time to go to the next level. Trust me, you'll love this."

"Did I ever tell you I was afraid of heights?" he asked, glancing down.

"Several times. Now just sit back in your harness like you're sitting into your sofa."

Cautiously sinking his hips back into his waist harness, he could feel the rope tighten. Realizing it would actually keep him from falling, he let out a big breath of built-up fear. "My philosophy has always been to go ahead and take risks," he said. "I just need to know that everything will turn out okay."

"Remember—to lower yourself down slowly, lift your right hand and the rope will slide through the rappel device," I instructed. Little by little he began to move downward. About ten feet later a huge smile spread across his face. He looked below and shouted, "Oh shit! This is crazy! I love it!"

A few moments later Jim touched the ground. Once he was off the rope, I hooked in my waist harness and rappelled down to congratulate him with a big, backslapping hug.

"Thank you, thank you, thank you! I feel like a new man. No—I am a new man! What a rush!"

Jim is a perfect example of how a single courageous moment—in his case, picking up a phone and calling me for help—can transform a person and help him build success upon success.

You'll learn more about Jim's saga later. He not only changed his body, he also transformed his life.

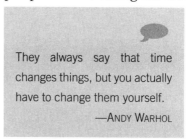

They always say that time changes things, but you actually have to change them yourself.

—ANDY WARHOL

Good-bye Old School

Don't get stuck believing that you have to follow yesterday's "rules" to guarantee your success today. You see, people tend to resist or fear any idea or behavior that threatens their existing beliefs. Recently I read about the research of a Canadian neurosurgeon who discovered some fascinating facts about the human mind's reaction to change. His experiments proved that when a person is forced to alter a fundamental belief or opinion, the brain reacts with a series of agonizing nervous sensations. Ouch! Here I'm talking about the courage for change and your brain is moaning, "Torture! Torture!"

Maybe that's why a lot of folks believe that only when suffering is more painful than change, they will think and act differently. But why wait—and why suffer?

When you don't develop your courage for change, you end up struggling.

When you develop your courage for change, you have the ability to succeed.

Work Your Courageous Maximus

Like any muscle, if you don't use your courage it won't get stronger. On the other hand, the more you exercise it the stronger it will become. This is what I've seen happen with everyone who takes a scary step toward living the life they really want. But scary is okay, because on the other side of fear is courage.

I learned this lesson from Jim's experience. Something told me to call him back one more time even though my "policy" was to stop after three calls. It was uncomfortable for me to make the fourth. I was afraid that I'd seem needy, desperate, and obnoxious. But another part of me insisted, Do it, Rich. This guy wants your help! I'm so glad I had the courage to follow my intuition, because the outcome was successful for me as well as for Jim.

If you want to improve your life, the courage for change is a prerequisite. Believe me, I know how frightening change can be. Making a big shift can tweak you out more than hanging off a cliff or jumping out of an airplane.

I know how hard it can be to leave a job that's bringing you consistent income but zero satisfaction. I know how uncomfortable it can feel when you realize that you have to leave your friends and family and move more than three thousand miles away to follow your dreams. I know how terrifying it can be to ask someone to marry you even though you've been dumped by two previous fiancées.

I've personally lived through all of the above, and every time I needed more and more courage. But what really matters is that I was willing to make changes in my life—even though I wasn't guaranteed a positive outcome.

That's why participating in extreme sports has changed

me in a very positive way. I would be a different person now if I'd never pushed my physical and mental limits. Thanks to my extreme adventures, I have gained confidence, courage, focus, and a "go for it" attitude.

Many times I've said to myself, If I can jump out of a plane, I can do this! (Whatever "this" might be.)

No—you don't have to sign up for the Ironman competition or climb on a mountain bike for the Kamikaze Downhill Race. What you do need to do is tap into the courage you already possess and develop it even more to overcome new situations and scary challenges.

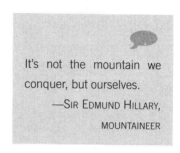

It's not the mountain we conquer, but ourselves.
—Sir Edmund Hillary,
MOUNTAINEER

You Have What It Takes

Making changes to improve your life doesn't have to feel like punishment, which is why I ask a lot of questions. Answering them will help you reach a higher level of self-awareness and allow you to base changes on *your* agenda.

As we move forward, I'm going to ask you even more questions that will help you clarify your most important dreams and

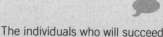

The individuals who will succeed and flourish will also be masters of change: adept at reorienting their own and others' activities in untried directions to bring about higher levels of achievement.
—Rosabeth Moss Kanter,
AUTHOR AND HARVARD
BUSINESS SCHOOL PROFESSOR

goals. (In chapter 12 you'll learn how to turn your fear of change into an energizing force for success.)

By "training your brain" you can develop your ability to understand what change might bring you. The purpose is to alter your approach to change by challenging the beliefs and opinions that may be holding you back from success.

As the saying goes, If you keep doing what you've always done, you'll keep getting what you always got. In order to get what you really want, you must be willing to change—and that may mean being uncomfortable for a while.

It's up to you to muster your courage. I *know* you have what it takes to do it.

Reality Check

What is the scariest or most uncomfortable thing you've ever done?

_____

How has that change affected your success?

_____

What is a change you could make in your life *right now* that you've been avoiding because it is scary or uncomfortable?

_____

What are you afraid of? (Name the small and the big things.)

_____

How might this change affect your future success?

I'm not asking you to take any action right now. I just want you to check your fear meter before we move ahead. We'll come back to these questions in chapter 12 when we discuss how to turn fear into success.

Keepers: Thoughts to Remember

➤ A single courageous moment can transform your life.

➤ Courage is like a muscle.

➤ On the other side of fear is courage.

➤ If you want to improve your life, you must develop the courage for change.

➤ When you develop the courage for change, you pave the way to struggle-free success.

➤ Courage comes from within. It is always available to you. All you have to do is tap into it, expand on it, and take action.

Action Idea #6: Stop Kidding Yourself

Invest the next few minutes at your keyboard or in a journal to answer the question: Where in my life might I be kidding myself? Pause for a moment and be 100 percent honest. By peering deep inside yourself, you will find the answer. (I've heard many different responses to this question, such as: health, a tough conversation with a friend or loved one, addictions, etc.) Again, I'm not asking you to take any further action right now. I just want you to be aware before we move ahead.

Action Idea #7: Find Your Courage

Here's a powerful technique that can help you build your natural courage: Bring to mind an experience when you took action even though you were scared. It helps to pinpoint a specific time when this happened. Got it? As you think about that moment of courage, recall how you felt.

It doesn't matter if the outcome was successful or not. It's that moment of courage that you want to remember. Take some time to really experience what it felt like.

Now think of a recent time when this same type of internal courage might have helped you face a situation that was frightening or uncomfortable. What might have been different if you had used this courage? Hold on to this feeling and bring to mind a change that you have been resisting or avoiding.

Imagine that your courage is giving you all the strength you need to go for it, that you are so confident that nothing can stop you from taking on this challenge. Feel the new connection you have to your courage. Notice how it flows through your body and how you begin to breathe deeper and feel more solid. This courage comes from within. It is always available to you. All you have to do is to tap into it, expand on it, and take action.

5

→

You're Not Stuck With "You"

Most Americans do not know what their strengths are. When you ask them, they look at you with a blank stare, or they respond in terms of subject knowledge, which is the wrong answer.

—Peter F. Drucker

My arms felt like they were being yanked out of my torso. "You're gonna get wrecked, Rich!" my inner voice screamed. "Just let go. You don't want to end up a Venus di Milo impersonator, do you?" I actually yelled out, "No! I can get this." Then, all of a sudden—*whoosh!*—I was up, riding on the wakeboard. My fingers squeezed the towrope as water hit me in the face and a big grin spread across my face. "I'm wakeboarding!" I shouted.

Then—*splash!* I fell forward and landed facefirst as what seemed like a gallon of river water gushed down my throat. Okay. I'm getting this, I said to myself, gagging. This is kind of like skateboarding or unicycling. I just have to find my center of balance.

After the boat turned around and I clutched the towrope again, I focused on the balancing skills I had developed years before. When I was in my early teens I could either be found riding my skateboard at the Wooden Wave skate park or pedaling my unicycle up and down homemade ramps in the driveway.

"Hit it!" I shouted. The boat's motor screamed with a throaty rumble. As the rope pulled, I held my body position firm as the wakeboard wedged its way through the water. Then I popped up on my feet. I did it! I was cruising along, feeling my center of balance, and riding the board like a magic carpet.

My friends G (remember him, the karate champ?) and Boomer, were standing up in the boat watching me with their fists held high in the air. When they had asked me if I wanted to try wakeboarding for the first time, I said yes without hesitation. I had water-skied before, but this was different. First off, I was standing sideways on this thing that looked like a giant skateboard with booties bolted to it. And I felt like I was floating! Because the board was about four feet long and almost two feet wide, it rode on top of the wake instead of cutting through it like a water ski. I loved it!

After three runs, I was surfing the wake and letting go of the rope's handle with one hand so I could give the hang-loose sign to my buds. Then I cut across the wake and jumped a couple of feet in the air. My skateboarding and unicycling techniques were paying off!

Then another skill came to mind. I used to practice front flips over and over on a trampoline and when I bungeed. As I jumped the wake again I thought, I bet I can pull off a front flip. I was riding the board on the right side of the wake, so I leaned hard to the left, skimmed toward the big wake at leg-shaking speed, bent my knees, and then let out a big "yeeeaahhhh!" as I launched into a full front flip. I made it all the way around and landed on the board. Then I took a sideways roll, the rope ripped out of my hands, and I skipped across the water on my back before coming to a floating stop. Awesome!

Boomer later told me that no one goes for a front flip on his or her first day out. It's an advanced move reserved for veterans. I'm glad no one had told me that before I thought about trying it.

Once again, I learned how to achieve success in a new activity by redirecting acknowledged strengths and skills toward it.

That's why I know that it's essential to face goals with the knowledge that you already possess the instruments of success without struggle.

> To overcome limitations is to experience the full delight of success.
>
> —ARTHUR SCHOPENHAUER

"It's Just the Way I Am"

At our initial coaching session, where Mike and I reviewed his history, goals, values, and challenges in order to customize our coaching partnership, he talked to me straight. "I've been to a bunch of personal development workshops. I've listened to the tapes and read all the books. I've got this info coming out of my ears." Nevertheless, Mike, at twenty-eight, was still smoking and drinking every day and his bad health habits made him feel terrible. He'd sunk into credit card debt by a hefty $30,000. His company, which produced TV commercials, was making only $50,000 per year and taking so much of his time that his four-year-old daughter barely knew him.

Mike knew exactly what to do, but he wasn't doing it. "I've never been good at follow-through. It's just the way I am. I don't even floss my teeth!" he whined. Stuck in self-sabotage,

Mike was buying into the internal lie that he was genetically programmed for failure. He was also beating himself up with the "should"s.

"I should be working smarter," he said. "I should be a better parent. I should take better care of my health. I should stick to a higher-level clientele and not accept small deals." Instead of clarifying what kind of client he really wanted, he'd accept any job that came down the pike. Where goals were concerned, he would start off all fired up, then he would burn out fast.

Mike was selling out on himself because he thought he couldn't change. "Mike, stop, 'shoulding' on yourself! You keep telling me that you *should* be doing these things and at the same time you're telling me that you can't do them because it's just the way you are? That's bull! You're basing your beliefs on what *hasn't* worked instead of on what *might* work. Tell me: What is one thing that you do well?"

"I'm really good at keeping my word with people," he answered. Mike was right. He *was* a master at creating and deepening relationships. When I asked him to rate the friends and community area of his life on a scale of 1 to 10, he gave it a 9.5.

"Since keeping your word with others is so important to you, how about if we put that same priority on keeping your word with yourself? So far you keep sending a message to yourself that you can't be trusted. Let's set up some achievable steps that you can commit to taking. Then each week, a big part of my job will be to hold up an imaginary mirror so you can see how you are keeping your word."

Mike squirmed a little in his chair, but I knew I hit a home run when he acknowledged, "That is exactly what I need: to honor myself as well as I honor other people. I'm ready to do this. You have my word."

I smiled and said, "I'm glad to hear that *you* have your word."

To begin, Mike made a commitment not to use his credit cards and sealed them in an envelope that read DO NOT TOUCH. If he ever got the urge to tear into that envelope, he promised to call me first. In time, he built up the courage to say no to certain jobs that weren't worth his time. He began to focus on high-end clients. Taking on his life in small bites—and accepting accountability for those bites—enabled Mike to make huge changes. After six weeks he cut his smoking down to three days per week and then to nothing without beating himself up for not going cold turkey right away. Over six months he cut back his drinking to once a week, if that.

As we go through this book, we'll follow Mike's progress. You'll see what happens as he changes his previous self-imposed limitation ("I've never been good at follow-through. It's just the way I am") to his new, self-developed understanding ("I do what I say I will do").

Weakness Is Just an Underdeveloped "Muscle"

Right about now you may be thinking, But Rich—you don't know me. Sure, I'm good at some things—but I find it hard to believe that they can lead me to perpetual success.

Let me give you another example from my own life. Recently my mom mailed me a box filled with my report cards and progress reports from elementary school through high school. At least a dozen of those assessments had the same box checked: "Lacks the motivation to succeed."

I remember that it sure was tempting to give in to that belief. When I was eight years old, I was diagnosed as "hyperki-

netic." My parents were told I had attention deficit disorder
(ADD). Staying focused was really tough. I was disorganized,
and my handwriting consistently looked like I had just downed
twelve cups of coffee. For years I told myself I was destined
to be a failure.

When I decided to become a bodybuilder, I was very
aware of my weaknesses. But I also knew I had a powerful
strength: commitment. Using this asset I learned how to set
achievable goals. Here's what I did:

1. I found an inspiring role model: Arnold Schwarzenegger. I
learned all about how he built his body and followed his
techniques for physical and mental progress.

2. I set achievable goals, such as what my body-fat percentage
would be and how much weight I would bench press.

3. I took consistent action and had a workout partner to help
me stay focused and accountable. (See chapter 7 for the
power of partnership.)

It worked! I was a competitive bodybuilder for ten years,
building "muscle" by redirecting a strength to an area where
I wanted to succeed. In the past I didn't know how to set
goals or get organized. I didn't know how beneficial a partner
could be. But now I did. I applied the techniques I developed
to many other areas of my life, like earning a college degree
and building a business. In the process, I compensated for—
and overcame—my weak spots.

I even applied the same technique to my sloppy handwriting and messy desk. Finding an inspiring model of beautiful
handwriting on an architect's floor plan, I copied the precise

printing until I had it down, with my own personal touch, of course. I set achievable goals of cleaning up my office, and I listened to lots of tapes and read books on how to be organized. Most important, I stayed consistent with it. I maintain a clean office by having my Success Partner ask me each week, "What is your office satisfaction level on a scale of one to ten?" That keeps me from letting things go beyond the point of no return. Today, I am proud of my handwriting, and I thrive in my clean office.

Now I look at other things I've been successful in and I ask myself, Okay, how did I create success there? What strengths did I have or learn that I can also apply to this new area? Then I redirect and apply those strengths to the new venture. Each success builds on the previous one.

You Already Have What You Need to Succeed

I have yet to meet a person who didn't feel he or she failed at *something*. At the same time, the same person always admitted to succeeding at something else.

Guess what? That area of success reflects strengths you own. These enormous assets can help you overcome those shortcomings you may think are holding you back from success.

Here's the thing: Most of your limits are self-imposed. You are *not* stuck with your personality and you are *not* stuck with your weaknesses.

You can use your current strengths to overcome your current weaknesses. "Weaknesses" are really just underdeveloped qualities. You don't have to give up on any of your dreams or goals just because you think you don't "have what it takes to succeed." Remember:

If you concentrate on your "weaknesses,"
you are going to struggle.
If you concentrate on your strengths,
you are going to succeed.

Right now, name three things at which you excel. What did it take to become great at them? Often we have natural strengths that we develop even more. As in sports, you'll never be great at something unless you practice. If you have a natural strength, one of the best things you can do is to focus on making it even stronger. That is, if you want to excel with that strength.

Now imagine redirecting those same skills, strategies, and/ or strengths to an area that you currently view as a weakness. This is the whole Extreme Success paradigm: You apply a winning technique from one experience to a very different one.

That's why I believe that most of your focus should be on developing your strengths so that you are superb at what you most love to do. This will make you stand out from the crowd and help you be more triumphant with less struggle and wasted energy. Also, if you put most of your energy into trying to improve your weaknesses, you might end up being good in lots of areas—but you might miss out on being great in others.

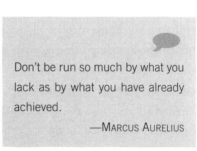

Don't be run so much by what you lack as by what you have already achieved.

—MARCUS AURELIUS

You Know What Your Strengths Are

Think "weaknesses" are holding you back? "Limitations" didn't stop these extreme achievers:

➤ Charles M. Schulz's cartoons were rejected by his high school yearbook staff.

➤ Robin Williams was voted Least Likely to Succeed in high school.

➤ Albert Einstein was four years old before he could speak and seven before he could read.

How Well Do You Know Yourself?

Make a list of ten of your top personal strengths (in no specific order). These can be character-based strengths, such as being thoughtful, honest, resourceful, or persuasive. They can also be skill-based strengths, such as being artistic, proficient at repairing things, or adept at a certain sport. If you're having a hard time completing this exercise or the one that follows, see the tips below.

1. _____

2. _____

3. _____

4. _____

5. _____

6. _____

7. _____

8. _____

9. _____

10. _____

Now list one to three of your most underdeveloped qualities or skills that might be holding you back from greater success. (Why not ten? Because I want you to focus more on what you *have* versus what you believe you're lacking. I don't want you to "dig" for weaknesses.)

1. _____

2. _____

3. _____

Want Some Help?

Here are a few tips to help you identify your strengths and weaknesses:

Take some time to think about your past accomplishments and create a mental (or written) list of things that you did well, enjoyed doing, and were proud of. Don't forget your education, training, volunteer opportunities, jobs, projects, school assignments, travel, and group activities. This can help you identify the natural assets you used to achieve these accomplishments.

Ask three of your family members, friends, or coworkers what they see as your top three personal strengths. They can help you identify ones that you may not have noticed. (This is a great self-esteem builder. Review this powerful list when you're feeling down on yourself.)

Then ask them to help you identify one weakness that would benefit you to overcome.

Need Some Ideas?

Listed below are a selection of positive traits. If you haven't identified ten strengths, use it. You can also refer to it to recognize weaknesses. How? Look at these strengths to see if you are drastically missing any of them and then think about what the opposite would be. For example: Do you severely lack the ability to be flexible, or organized, or daring? That probably means that you have a weakness such as being too rigid, or disorganized, or fearful.

observant	instructive	persistent	intuitive
dependable	objective	conceptual	adaptable
logical	flexible	shrewd	perceptive
honest	conscientious	astute	proficient
resourceful	genuine	daring	time management
energetic	forceful	creative	enthusiastic
detailed	persuasive	tactful	discerning
aggressive	diligent	reliable	adept

sincere	active	straightforward	consistent
loyal	demanding	thoughtful	strategic
effective	committed	methodical	imaginative
exacting	independent	productive	fair
broad-minded	systematic	analytical	good listener
problem solver	self-starter	highly motivated	organized
get results	motivate others	innovative	disciplined
goal oriented	physically fit	interpersonal skills	

Keepers: Thoughts to Remember

➤ Most of your limits are self-imposed.

➤ "Weaknesses" are really just underdeveloped qualities.

➤ You can achieve success in a new activity by redirecting your past strengths and skills toward it.

➤ If you concentrate on your "weaknesses," you are going to struggle. If you concentrate on your strengths, you are going to succeed with greater ease.

➤ If you have a natural strength, one of the best things you can do is to focus on making it even stronger.

➤ When you focus on developing your strengths so that you are superb at what you most love to do, you stand out from the crowd and are more successful with less struggle and wasted energy.

Action Idea #8: Apply Your Assets

Look at what you've been successful in and think about how you created success there. What strengths did you use or learn that you might also apply to your new goals? These enormous assets can help you overcome those shortcomings you may think are holding you back from success.

For example, if your weakness is trying to do everything on your own, look to the strong relationships you have established for help. Or, if you are fearful in a new job position, identify situations where you exhibited confidence and courage. What did you do to get that way? How could you use that same process to help you develop your courage in this new area? Each new success can build on the previous one.

Action Idea #9: Work Strength

Choose one underdeveloped quality that you would most like to change and write down at least one thing you could do to develop it. Don't forget to redirect one or more of your strengths that you identified in Action Idea #8.

Then make a personal commitment to work on developing this underdeveloped quality for the next thirty days. At the end of thirty days, reassess where you are.

6

Who Are You?

To attract attractive people, you must be attractive. To attract powerful people, you must be powerful. To attract committed people, you
must be committed. Instead of going to work on them, you go to work
on yourself. If you become, you can attract.

—Jim Rohn, *7 Strategies for Wealth & Happiness*

Several years ago I signed up for a ninety-day "Life Success
Course." There were fifteen participants, each of whom set
several personal and professional goals to achieve by the time
the program was completed.

In that course, I was instructed to create my own Personal
Contract, which is basically a one-sentence affirmation of the
qualities I most wanted to develop in myself in order to project a stronger personal presence.

My Personal Contract, which I had to create and say out
loud to myself, was "I am a lovable, vulnerable, and playful
man who's on fire!"

When I first heard about using a personal affirmation to
expand my personality, I didn't really buy it. I thought, How
can saying a few words over and over make any difference?

At the time self-protection was really important to me. If you've seen the movie *Good Will Hunting* you know that growing up in the Boston area can be tough. When I let myself be vulnerable back east it would often bring a comment from a friend like, "What are you—a wimp?" To avoid that insult, I told myself to hold back and not show my emotions. This attitude was pretty tough when it came to strangers, too. I felt uncomfortable meeting new people so I would be quiet and serious. Not only would I not let people see my feelings, sometimes—too often—I wouldn't even allow myself to feel.

So at first the Personal Contract was very strange to me. I didn't believe what I was saying. But after a couple weeks of repeating it I started to think, Maybe I *am* some of the contract. I kept repeating the message to myself.

About a year later I was taking a course at the Coaches Training Institute in San Rafael, California. In one of the learning exercises, the workshop of about thirty people was split into several groups of about five people each. We were instructed to tell each person in the group what qualities they exhibited that made him or her a great coach.

When it was my turn the other participants started to say things like, "Even though he is big and looks like he might be a tough guy, he is actually quite vulnerable," and "He seems very lovable. He definitely cares about people," and "I like how playful and enthusiastic he is."

I was blown away! Honestly, at first, I thought, Who's playing the joke here? Who told these guys about my personal contract? No one had. By affirming those qualities in myself, and by paying attention to them over the past year, the "real me" had been revealed—and people liked him! I had become my contract and my contract had become me! What I didn't realize when I first formed my Personal Contract, was that I actually *had* those assets—but I was hiding them from myself! That's why I instinctively picked the ones I did.

Over and over again with my coaching clients I have seen how saying a few specifically chosen words can make a dramatic positive impact on growing yourself as a person. Now I find myself praising the benefits of this "Success Ritual" when I speak and when I write (like right now!).

You Are What You Think

Often people tell themselves what they are *not*. "I'm not outgoing," "I'm not confident," "I'm not lovable," or "I'm not relaxed." When you constantly send messages like these to yourself, you end up believing them.

Flip a negative self-message and watch what happens. A more affirming message that you possess a positive value can help you expand who you *are*.

I've seen men and women purposely squelch their natural strengths because they were afraid that revealing them would make them look stupid, soft, or "uncool." Many of the qualities they struggle to suppress could actually help them be more successful. That's because tapping into your personality resources boosts your presence, helps you connect better with others, and im-

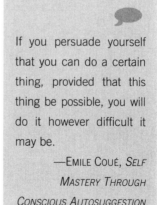

If you persuade yourself that you can do a certain thing, provided that this thing be possible, you will do it however difficult it may be.

—EMILE COUÉ, *SELF MASTERY THROUGH CONSCIOUS AUTOSUGGESTION*

proves your impact. By using these valuable assets you've been holding back, you can become more attractive, effective, and successful.

If you tell yourself negative things about yourself, you will struggle.

If you tell yourself positive things about yourself, you will see opportunities when they come and succeed.

It's Time to Balance Your Personality

Remember my client, Christine, who filled out the Life Balance Wheel? She's the financial adviser who wanted more balance in her life. After about three months, we scheduled an in-person coaching session to review her achievements and plan her next steps.

Christine's results were awesome. Her income was exceeding her best month ever by 30 percent! Now nineteen pounds thinner, she had allowed herself a week at a spa resort in Arizona, her first vacation in over three years. I acknowledged Christine for her commitment, focus, and willingness to trust the process and change her life for the better.

She replied, "It was a lot easier than I thought it would be. I didn't know why my life wasn't working, but now I can see it was a matter of priorities and choice."

Then I pulled out a new Life Balance Wheel and asked Christine to fill out the blank form. When she had completed it, I put this new form and her first form side by side (see next page).

As you can see, Christine's satisfaction rose in most areas. Her Life Balance Wheel was a lot steadier. However, I noticed that her level of satisfaction with her family and friends hadn't changed. And another area immediately got my no-

Christine's Life Balance Wheel
March

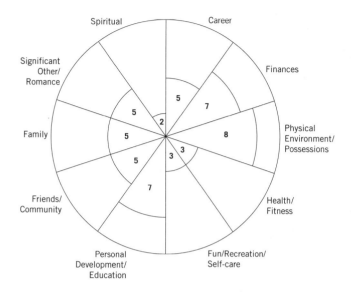

Christine's Life Balance Wheel
June

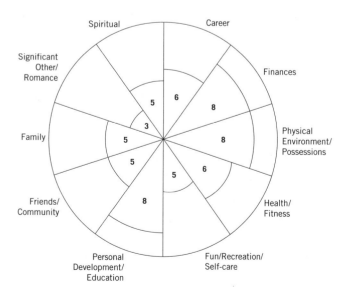

tice. I asked, "Why has romance dropped from a five to a three?"

"Well, a few months ago I felt insecure about my weight—as you know—so I didn't even care that much about dating," Christine told me. "What really mattered was feeling better about myself. Now that I've lost the pounds, I feel much better and I'd like to start dating again. But it's been so long since I've been on a date, I'm too nervous to do anything about it."

"Okay. How about friends and family? Anything you want to say about that?"

"I'm just not that happy with how they are treating me. My mom always phones me at work to chat, my sister keeps calling me at home to complain about her husband, and my friends want to go out for drinks almost every night. I feel like I have no time for me."

"Have you said anything to your mom, your sister, or your friends about this?"

"No. They really seem to need me and I can't let them down."

Affirming Success

I told Christine that she could benefit from a Personal Contract to help build her personal power. She agreed to give it a shot. It was clear that she felt insecure doing the dating scene, so she chose the word *confident*. We also figured out that she kept trying to take care of everyone in her life except for herself. She realized that she had to start speaking her truth instead of selling herself out just to be nice. Consequently she chose the words *bold* and *honest*.

We talked about the romance area a little more, and Christine admitted that she used to enjoy dating but now didn't feel like she had "it." When I asked her what "it" was, she told me that she didn't feel sexy anymore. "Ah, so we need to add *sexy* in your contract," I said.

"No way!" Christine snapped back. "I don't want to say I'm sexy out loud every day."

"It doesn't matter if you want to. What matters is that it might help you get what you want."

After a moment she nodded grudgingly.

"It's time to begin the process. I want you to state your contract to me. When I truly believe that you own what you're saying, when I really get that you're being authentic and not just acting, I'll stand up. If I don't truly get it, then I'm going to stay in my seat."

Christine nodded and confessed, "All the moisture from my mouth just traveled to the palms of my hands." Then, rocking back and forth in her chair, she mumbled, "I am a confident, sexy, and boldly honest woman who gets what she wants." Noticing I hadn't budged, she complained, "This is stupid. Do we *have* to do this?"

Without hesitation I said, "Do it again." She did. I still didn't move. "C'mon. That was pretty good," she tried to convince me.

"Christine, do you really believe that you have those qualities?"

"Uh . . . definitely."

"Then take a big breath and *own* those qualities. Realize that they *are* part of you. *Then* state your contract."

She closed her eyes, took a deep breath, opened her eyes to stare at me, and declared, "I *am* a confident, sexy, and boldly honest woman who gets what she wants." *Bam!* I jumped to my feet.

Christine smiled. "I see what you mean. That time I actually felt like these qualities were part of me."

"Yes!" I exclaimed. "Those qualities *are* part of you. When you believe it on the inside, it shows up on the outside. And you have to keep letting those qualities show up, because they bring out so much more of who you are."

Christine agreed to pronounce her Personal Contract at least once a day for the next thirty days. I also asked her to make sure that she said it out loud in a private place where no one would hear her (while driving in her car or in her bathroom at home).

A week later Christine told me that speaking her Personal Contract was a bit odd but she agreed to continue with the process. The next week she told me, "I actually *like* my contract now." A month later she told me that things had changed. While on a business trip she met a man who lived less than an hour from her home. They had already been on two dates and she was floating in the clouds!

Christine also used the message of her Personal Contract to tell her family members her bold truth. She asked her mom to call her after work only. She informed her sister that she no longer wanted to hear about her marital problems though she wanted to offer support. Focusing on solutions, not problems, was a better use of their time.

"It's like I was covered up so that no one would notice the real me," she told me later. "What a relief it is to say what I mean and mean what I say."

> Don't ask yourself what the world needs; ask yourself what makes you come alive. And then go and do that. Because what the world needs is people who have come alive.
>
> —HAROLD WHITMAN

My wife, Kathy, an actress and personal coach, is known for helping people achieve greater success by coaching them to be more authentic. In Kathy's workshops I've seen her students, who want to learn how to be more effective actors, expand their personal presence dramatically. In the process they also become more successful people. Why? Because they learn how to bring out more of who they really are.

Kathy finds it ironic that actors are called by that name. She says that in order to be a great actor, you must actually learn to let go of your act! You must remove the mask you wear. She calls actors "authenticity artists" instead.

It's really the nonactors who are the greatest performers. If you look closely, you can see ordinary people wearing custom-designed masks. You'll recognize the "Pleaser," the "Tolerator," the "Look Good," and the "Tough Guy" masks, just to name a few.

Years ago, when Kathy was a talent agent, she was an expert at wearing the "Look Good" mask. She had an impressive career and lots of money, a beautiful house on a fancy street lined with palm trees, a new car, and nice clothes. By most standards, she appeared successful.

But underneath that look-good image was a very different reality. She was lonely and sad. Divorced, with a nasty relationship with her ex, she was a single mom with no time for her child. A workaholic with papers piled high and phones ringing off the hook, she had had a series of unhealthy relationships after her divorce and no real friends. Fun was something other people had.

What she wanted more than anything was to be loved. And the way she thought she would accomplish this was by appearance. Yet the harder she tried to look good, the more she pushed people away. That's the problem with these masks. They don't get you what you really want.

When Kathy sold her agency to teach "authenticity artists," she discovered that it was the "real Kathy" that people wanted to see. As she slowly and courageously removed her mask and became more real, honest, and vulnerable, she started to connect with others on a much deeper level.

Today she knows how much I love her. We both have an excellent friendship with her ex-husband, she has a deep connection with her two children, and enjoys a group of friends who are as close as family.

Taking off the mask works!

People wear masks because they mistakenly think that who they are is not enough, and that in order to get what they want they need to put on a good act. The opposite is true. Whether you want closer relationships, higher sales, or a bigger presence, you will become more successful by being real.

Kathy's Lessons:

1. If you wear a mask that you think will be acceptable to others, you betray your real self.
2. Masks create barriers and do not get you what you want.
3. Being receptive and genuine will expand your personal presence and can connect you with others instantly!

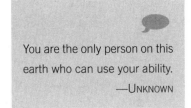

You are the only person on this earth who can use your ability.

—UNKNOWN

Reality Check

Answer the following questions for a better understanding of who you are and how you operate.

Quick—answer this question: What mask do you sometimes wear to protect yourself?

_____

What are you specifically trying to conceal? What are you afraid of?

_____

What benefits might you gain by allowing others to see that part of you?

_____

If you were being totally real, how would you describe yourself? What would you be like? How would you be acting differently?

_____

Your answers can help you gain clarity about what qualities you have been suppressing. They can also give you a better idea of what qualities to include in your Personal Contract.

Keepers: Thoughts to Remember

➤ When you send negative messages to yourself, you end up believing them.

➤ If you tell yourself positive things about yourself, you will see opportunities when they come to you and you'll use more of your natural strengths, connect better with others, and improve your impact. By using these valuable assets you've been holding back, you can become more attractive and effective.

➤ If you wear a mask, take it off. You will become more real and will start to connect with others on a much deeper level. Being real means being successful.

Action Idea #10: Find the Real You

Create your own Personal Contract. Write down a one-sentence affirmation of the qualities you most want to develop and bring out. Remember: Choose personal traits you have been hiding, even if that means getting uncomfortable. This is about balancing your personality by bringing out more of the real you.

You might want to refer back to the list of personal traits on page 86 for ideas. If you asked your friends, family, and coworkers to help you discover your strengths and weaknesses from the exercise in chapter 5, that information may help, too. If you didn't ask anyone for input, maybe now is a good time to do so. Often the people around you can identify what you are not seeing for yourself.

After you create your contract, state it out loud to yourself several times a day for thirty days. Speak your Personal Contract with as much feeling as possible.

Over time you will become even more of the person you truly want to be. You'll gain a better focus on where and how you can improve yourself to bring out all you are. After thirty days, notice how your Personal Contract works for you.

Want Some Ideas?

Here are some examples of Personal Contracts.

➤ I am a powerful, focused, and bold leader who inspires people and gets results.

➤ I am a playful, fun-loving, and exciting woman who gets the most out of life.

➤ I am a talented, trusting, and creative artist who expects and accepts unlimited abundance.

➤ I am a caring, handsome, and confident man who deserves a loving relationship.

➤ I am a relaxed, intuitive, and spiritual woman who honors herself and others.

➤ I am a conscious, curious, and open-minded man who listens to others with wonder.

➤ I am a disciplined, focused, and organized businessperson who is achieving unlimited success without struggle.

➤ I am an honest, caring, and convincing salesperson who people listen to and respect.

➤ I am a wild and crazy guy who loves to have fun!

PART 3

PART 3

Don't Climb Alone

7

One Is a Struggle, Two Is a Breeze

No man [or woman] can achieve greatness alone.
—Napoleon Hill, author of *Think & Grow Rich*

Recently I was hired to give a keynote speech at an annual convention in Vancouver. My wife, Kathy, joined me, so we added a few vacation days to the trip. As usual, I asked the locals where we could find the best rock climbing. We were told to head for Squamish Valley, British Columbia's Yosemite.

Squamish was an amazing site of polished-smooth, towering granite cliffs, which meant steep and challenging climbs. It was a cold, windy day in a totally new environment, and I could feel my adrenaline begin to kick in.

Kathy stood at the base of the cliff working the rope that was attached to my waist harness. Her job was to let rope out, or take it in, to match my progress as I climbed the sheer cliff. If I fell, it was up to Kathy to stop me.

About halfway up, I hit an impasse. I had to make a difficult move, and in trying to figure it out, my mind suddenly clicked into a spiral-thinking pattern that spun me off track.

I worried that if I fell, Kathy—who is half my size—

wouldn't be able to hold me and stop my fall. From that point on, my thoughts engulfed me in a tidal wave of indecision. The rope might break; I didn't have enough protective gear; and on and on. My legs began to tremble. My jaw clenched. My breathing became frantic and tense. Stuck in the Struggle Syndrome, I was freaking out! Kathy must have sensed my dilemma, because at that moment her voice broke through the storm raging inside my head.

"How do you feel up there?" she shouted.

That's all it took to snap me out of the "I'm-gonna-fall-and-my-protection-will-fail-and-the-rope-will-break-and-I-will-hit-the-ground" spell I had plunged into. It was like she turned on a light so I could see reality. I took a deep breath, put a big smile on my face, and looked down.

"I feel good now. Thanks for bringing me back to my senses."

I reeled in my crazy thoughts, trusting that if I did fall Kathy would catch me, as she'd done on other climbs. Telling myself that the rope had never broken and our safety measures and protective gear had always come through, I repositioned my body, took another deep breath, pushed up, and made the move.

She pulled me out of the Struggle Syndrome by helping me stop, be aware, and resume control. She knew what to say that would prompt me to take action.

On this climb, Kathy was my Success Partner. One of her roles was to give me feedback—really a "wake-up" call that snapped me out of my downward mental spiral. It may seem like a simple thing, but if Kathy

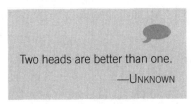

Two heads are better than one.
—UNKNOWN

hadn't asked me how I was feeling, I might not have been able to reassess my situation and climb through it.

Excuse Me, But . . .

Success Partners possess the power to interrupt distracting thought patterns. Left to our own devices, we'll sit spinning our wheels in the rut of day-to-day routine. Success Partners provide solid traction by asking simple questions like, "Hey! What's the reality here?" or "What's one small thing you can do this week to move your plan forward?" A Success Partner can breathe new life into a stalled plan by adding accountability for your action—or nonaction.

What would it be like to see yourself without all the limitations you've taken for granted? That's what a Success Partner does, because she doesn't experience the same fear of failure and rejection that you do. And because she doesn't undergo your worries first hand, she has the uncanny ability to push you to greater heights. Remember: Success is often waiting on the other side of a self-imposed limitation.

That's Easy for You to Say

Exactly! It's *much* easier for a Success Partner to see you in an objective light, allowing him or her to tell you like it is. A Success Partner can nudge you toward what you truly want, instead of allowing you to accept what you think you deserve. In this way, a partner becomes your champion who reminds you of your past successes and shows you how to apply them to your current situation. Simply put, your Success Partner can act as the echo of your own ideals and goals. He or she can pry you out of your comfort zone by challenging you to take action on important issues. A Success Partner can boost your confidence, courage, and faith in yourself.

> There is more to us than we know. If we can be made to see it, perhaps, for the rest of our lives, we will be unwilling to settle for less.
>
> —KURT HAHN, FOUNDER OF OUTWARD BOUND

Think of it this way: Your Success Partner not only turns up your personal "awareness light"—one that you may have turned down low—he makes it his job to illuminate what you are not seeing in yourself.

Strength in Numbers

One of the joys of living on the Pacific Coast is being able to hike through its amazing redwood forests. A few years ago I went on my first tour of Muir Woods near San Francisco, which is one of California's many redwood "cathedrals." After hiking for a few minutes, our group came to a clearing in the midst of a grove of towering, ancient sequoias. Shafts of sunlight poured down through the tops of the trees, and as I peered up I could barely see where these amazing columns ended and the sky began.

Our tour guide told us that although redwoods can grow incredibly high, some of them soaring hundreds of feet skyward, their roots sink down into the earth less than six feet. All the redwoods spread out their roots and interlock with each other. By doing this they support each other from toppling over when they reach new heights or when strong winds howl through the forest.

That is the power of partnership!

Humans are like redwood trees. We are strong and resourceful on our own, but when we combine our strengths with those of others, we can achieve greater "heights" with less effort. When we partner with others, we gain the support and structure to help us learn and grow even higher and stronger.

There's No Such Thing as a Self-Made Success

Sometimes we lose sight of what partnership can mean for us and those around us. As a professional coach, I've worked with and spoken to thousands of people. All of them came to me for one reason: They needed specific assistance and support that they couldn't find. Citing goals they wanted to accomplish, they didn't know where else to turn for help.

As I listened to their stories, I began to see that a fundamental need was not being met. People thrive with feedback, accountability, structure, and support. Without these incentives, success is tough to achieve. Here's why:

1. *Feedback* allows you to see new perspectives.
2. *Accountability* helps you take action.
3. *Structure* provides the plan to follow through on that action.
4. *Support* keeps you going until the goal is accomplished.

When you hook up with a Success Partner, sharing these actions helps you both to:

➤ move toward goals with greater ease;

➤ act on choices or decisions;

➤ develop new skills that translate into more success;

➤ tune in to your intuition and remain true to yourself and your values;

➤ accomplish things that seemed unattainable;

➤ acquire a sense of satisfaction in your experiences.

Pretty neat, huh? That's why working with a Success Partner makes sense. This connection clarifies what you want and prepares you for it. And when you find yourself at the intersection where strategy meets opportunity, a partnership shines a spotlight on those options. It is a vital element in making you a "luckier" person and bringing you closer to your desired goals.

Partners also acknowledge you when you really need it, that is, when you are least likely to do it for yourself. If you're feeling down on yourself, your partner can highlight your strengths and reinforce who you really are. These reminders can pick you up and get you back on the path to Extreme Success ASAP.

Research has shown that one behavior of those who are successful at making changes is that they utilize excellent support systems. But for some reason, many people tell themselves they are going to generate changes but don't tell anyone else about their plans. They do this—either consciously or unconsciously—in the dark because they are afraid of being viewed as a failure if the plan doesn't work out.

That's a shame, because sharing goals will get you to—and keep you on—the path to Extreme Success.

So consider:

When you go it alone, you struggle.

When you form a Success Partnership, both of you benefit by setting and achieving goals with more joy and ease.

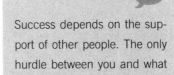

Success depends on the support of other people. The only hurdle between you and what you want to be is the support of others.

—David Joseph Schwartz

The Mastermind Principle

If you could lift a thirty-pound dumbbell with your left arm and a thirty-pound dumbbell with your right arm, reason and logic would have it that you could lift a sixty-pound barbell with both arms working together. In reality, you could actually lift an eighty-pound barbell! That is the principle of synergy. That is the principle of partnership. That is the principle of the Mastermind.

When two people bring their minds together to work on a positive goal synergy happens. There is, in a sense, a "third mind" that is greater than the parts that came together. Extra strength is discovered, and that creates momentum. One or both of the individual minds can use this third, or master, mind.

Have you ever experienced this phenomenon when exchanging ideas with someone? You get an idea, your friend adds to it, and then you enhance it. Together you come up with a terrific concept that neither of you had thought of on your own.

This is one of the greatest benefits of a Success Partnership. Meeting to discuss ideas, goals, and plans will allow you both to benefit from the Mastermind Principle. On our own, we can only come up with so many questions to ask ourselves. When a Success Partner asks new questions, he or she often allows us to bring new answers to light.

The Mastermind Principle has been known for hundreds, even thousands of years, yet today it is often overlooked. This is a shame, because the foundation of the Mastermind Principle is harmony.

Working in harmony with your Success Partner, you both experience exceptional results such as greater awareness, better focus, and improved motivation. Your partnership also becomes a magnet that helps attract the dreams and goals you share with each other. The stronger the connection you have with your partner, the more powerful the magnet will be.

My First Partner

My childhood diagnosis of ADD branded me an underachiever. I seemed destined to live out my academic career in the slow lane. School was not a friendly place, especially when I was continually assigned to classes everyone said were for the "dummies." By the time I reached the eighth grade, I pretty much agreed with the kids who heckled me. I was just plain stupid; I wouldn't amount to anything.

High school was a *major* bummer. Late in my senior year I learned that I wouldn't graduate with my class because I had failed English. Instead of the killer graduation party I was looking forward to, I faced a long, hot summer of make-up classes. But then something happened that changed my life.

My best friend Jima—we had been pals since middle school—asked me if I'd consider teaming up as his workout buddy and start lifting weights. Severely overweight (he weighed 255 pounds by the seventh grade) Jima, like me, was laboring under a heavy load of self-esteem challenges.

We came to an agreement and set up a schedule. Every other day, we met in the basement of his apartment complex and supported each other in our weight-lifting program. We set goals, like how much we wanted to weigh and how much iron we planned to lift.

It was incredible! As our bodies responded to the workouts, so did our self-esteem. I also learned some very important lessons, such as how to set compelling goals, stay focused and committed, and achieve an outcome.

Most of all, I discovered the power of a successful partnership. Had it not been for Jima's support, I never would have stuck to my weight-lifting program, much less eventually becoming a national-level competitive bodybuilder. As a team, we achieved more than we ever could have alone. I applied the same lessons to my educational goals. I partnered up with a fellow summer school student. We set weekly study goals and helped each other when we didn't understand an assignment. I passed the English course and earned my high school diploma. Now I chuckle when I think of how my high school English teacher will react when he sees that I'm a published author.

So Where Are *You*, Partner?

Put an X next to the statements that express how you really feel.

_____ Powerful people don't need support to achieve success.

_____ I rarely ask for help, because I don't want to "bug" anyone.

_____ I have never been one to ask for support or collaboration.

_____ If I ask someone for help, it makes me look weak.

_____ I rarely ask for help because it is easier to do things on my own.

_____ I have a hard time accepting help and support.

_____ I don't ask for help, because people always seem to let me down.

_____ I don't ask for help, because I want to do things _my_ way.

_____ I don't tell others my plans, because if I fail I don't want them to know.

_____ If I accept help from others, they might expect help from me.

_____ I don't have time to set up a supportive partnership with someone.

_____ If I get a Success Partner, I might actually have to take action on achieving my dreams and goals. That's a scary thought!

Scoring

Each X above counts for one point. Add up your X's and see how your opinions are affecting you.

0: You obviously understand the power of partnership and you're probably creating success with greater effectiveness and ease than most people. Keep it up and check out the next chapter to see how you can take your partnerships to the next level.

1 to 4: It looks like you are open to the idea of using partners to help you succeed. Most people I've worked with (myself included!) have encountered some types of obstacles when they asked for or offered support in their past. Challenge yourself to learn from your past and continue to expand the partnership skills that will help you reach new heights.

5 to 8: It's possible that you're making things harder than they need to be. You might also be stuck in what feels like a "comfort zone." That is, you're used to lacking the support needed to become a more successful person. Try a new perspective. Imagine what it would be like if several people were there for you 100 percent. Picture them championing you, offering helpful ideas, and connecting you with the people you most want to meet. Think about them assisting you to notice opportunities that you are not aware of. All that would make things easier, wouldn't it?

9 to 12: The Lone Ranger comes to mind here! You're probably working harder than you need to and getting less effective results. There's a good chance that you're not as focused as you could be. You probably won't learn much from this test that you haven't already suspected. You have been committed to "doing it" on your own for whatever the reason.

For some people, it's not always easy to ask for help. In an era of high divorce rates, many children don't see the positive side of partnership. Family and friends might be viewed as having "agendas." Still others experience feelings of guilt or defeat when they think of asking for support.

Assessing yourself this way may encourage you to take new action. So question your beliefs, especially those about asking for and getting support. Maybe partnerships didn't work well for you in the past, but trust me: With the right tools and partners, you'll be able to achieve Extreme Success without struggle.

Jill's Dilemma

That's what happened with Jill. Her public image had always been that of a strong, independent woman who gave aid much more often than she asked for it. She doled out so much support that she was on caregiver overload. But requesting assistance just didn't fit the image she wanted to project. She said it made her appear weak and left her feeling as though she was giving up. Still, she hired me because, as she explained, "You'll give me the support I need and I won't have to 'give' anything back. This is business." Working with me allowed her to focus on her life and accept unconditional support without judgment.

Over the course of a year, Jill took the time to research and purchase her first rental property. She also hired a housecleaner (thereby overcoming the conviction instilled by her mother that a woman should clean her own home). Also, she began doing yoga every day—something new for her—and toned up her body as she calmed her mind. Finally, she developed three meaningful new friendships.

Professionally, her life changed, too. She received the best review and biggest raise she had ever gotten in seven years at her company. No longer a Lone Ranger, Jill learned how partnership could make her life more fulfilled and successful.

Keepers: Thoughts to Remember

SUCCESS PARTNERSHIPS PROVIDE:

1. feedback, which allows you to see new perspectives;
2. accountability, which helps you to take action;
3. structure, which provides the plan to follow through on that action;
4. support, which keeps you going until the goal is accomplished.

➤ When you form a Success Partnership, both of you benefit by setting and achieving goals with more joy and ease. When you go it alone, you struggle.

➤ Partners acknowledge you when you really need it; that is, when you are least likely to do it for yourself.

➤ Synergy happens when two people bring their minds together to work on a positive goal. They create the Mastermind, a "third mind" that is greater than the parts that came together.

Action Idea #11: Know the Value of Partnership

This exercise can show you how a Success Partnership can work. Just think how friends and associates have already given you feedback, accountability, structure, and support. Jot down the names of three people in your life who have helped you to be more successful.

1. _____

2. _____

3. _____

Now write down how they did it.

1. _____

2. _____

3. _____

Great! Now you're more prepared to ask others for encouragement and support, because you have a better idea of what has worked well for you in the past.

In the next chapter I'll show you how to set up a Success Partnership with step-by-step instructions to help you take action on and stay focused on your goals.

8

A Partner for Success

Doing nothing for others is the undoing of ourselves.

—Horace Mann, historian and teacher

Partners are crucial for achieving extreme success. So let's look at *how* to form a Success Partnership and make it most effective as you move toward your personal and professional goals.

Are You Ready for a Success Partner?

Before you take another step, it is important that you are prepared for a Success Partner. You should be able to answer yes to the following statements.

1. I believe that this is the right time for me to have and to be a Success Partner, because I'm ready and willing to reach my potential.

2. I can be relied upon to be on time for our calls and/or meetings.

3. I will do my best, but I won't try to be perfect.

4. I will tell the truth to my Success Partner.

5. I will speak up if I feel that I'm not getting what I want from our partnership. I will share this information with my Success Partner as soon as I am aware of it.

Obviously, the person you choose is an important decision. You want to select someone whom you trust, can count on, and want to support, and who has a similar desire to do the same for you.

Name three potential people who you could ask to be your Success Partner.

1. _____

2. _____

3. _____

"Would You Like to Be Success Partners?"

Now it's time to ask someone from your list to be your Success Partner. Here's what you can say:

I'm reading a book that explains how people can become Success Partners and help each other get clear, take action, and stay focused on their most important goals. When I thought about who would be a great fit to be my Success Partner, I thought of you. Are you interested in doing this with me?

Here are ten questions that can determine if you're both ready to form a Success Partnership.

1. What do you want to get from our partnership?

2. Do you feel that we have the trust to fully support each other?

3. Why *me* as your Success Partner?

4. What works best for you as far as support?

5. What doesn't work for you as far as support?

6. How do you want to meet? (In person, by phone, or a mix of the two?)

7. How often do you want to meet? (Daily, weekly, biweekly, monthly?)

8. How do you want to stay in contact between our meetings? (E-mail, voice mail, fax, etc.)

9. What are the main goals you'd like to focus on?

10. Is there anything else you want to say? (This is always a good question to ask just to make sure that nothing is left unsaid.)

Once you've chosen a Success Partner (and before your first meeting) suggest that he or she read the previous chapters so that you're both on the same page (so to speak). That way, the mutual benefits of your collaboration will be really clear. Then you may want to agree to read one chapter each week between your meetings.

"Great! We're Success Partners . . . Now What?"

When you and a partner decide to support each other's goals, a big step in designing your alliance will be your first meeting. Whether in person or by telephone, this is the occasion to establish what you each want. It is the time to develop your connection and trust with each other, find out what you both want to focus on, and to "customize" your relationship to best meet your mutual needs. There are four steps to follow:

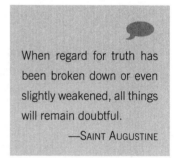

When regard for truth has been broken down or even slightly weakened, all things will remain doubtful.
—SAINT AUGUSTINE

_____ Step 1: Create Connection and Trust

_____ Step 2: Clarify What You Want

_____ Step 3: Prepare with a Success Partnership Form (SPF)

_____ Step 4: Develop Your Partnership Skills

Step 1: Create Connection and Trust

This first and perhaps most important step is the core of your relationship. You both need to feel free to open up and share your fears, challenges, and joys. One of the best ways to do this is to discuss your individual needs and concerns. Even if you and your Success Partner are already linked as friends and you trust each other, the simple act of discussing these subjects will make this essential foundation even stronger. Trust cannot be taken for granted—it must be built.

Here's how a conversation between two Success Partners (Kim and Rob) might go.

Kim: May I tell people that we're Success Partners?
Rob: Actually I'd prefer to keep it between us. What about you?
Kim: It's okay if you tell people that I'm your Success Partner.
Rob: I probably won't need to, but thanks, I'll remember that.
Kim: What else do you need in order to feel that we have the trust to say what's going on and to fully support each other?
Rob: What we just said does it for me. What about you?
Kim: I just want to know that whatever I say will stay between us unless I say it's okay to tell someone else.
Rob: Sure, you have my word. I would like the same agreement from you.
Kim: You've got it.
Rob: I feel complete with this. Is there anything else you need in order to feel that we have the trust to fully support each other?
Kim: No. This is great. Let's move forward.

These two partners have begun the process of communicating and asking for what they want from each other. As you can see, they have different confidentiality needs, but they have already deepened their trust and connection. The simple act of making an agreement and listening to each other's needs strengthens confidence and weakens doubt.

(Remember Jill from the last chapter? After about six months of coaching her, I taught her how to set up a Success Partnership, and she chose her sister, whom she trusted. They began meeting by phone once a week and in person once a month. Her sister helped her stay accountable to doing yoga and they still support each other in being more effective in their respective careers.)

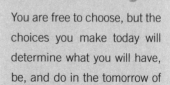

> You are free to choose, but the choices you make today will determine what you will have, be, and do in the tomorrow of your life.
>
> —Zig Ziglar, AUTHOR
> OF *Over the Top*

Step 2: Clarify What You Want

The second step is to share what you want. This is the time to voice your visions, values, goals, and fears.

By knowing them you can:

➤ help each other explain the most important steps to reach your goals;

➤ challenge each other to take bigger risks and hold each other accountable;

➤ pay better attention to lessons learned when one of you encounters a challenge or an obstacle;

➤ celebrate when either of you has a big win.

When I first meet with a client, I always ask for three primary areas he or she would like to focus on during the first three months of our partnership.

You can do the same thing with your Success Partner. For each focus area write a simple heading and under it a description of how to achieve it. Here's a sample.

Primary Focus

1. *Become financially responsible.* Set up a system to track my spending and income. Reconcile my bank accounts each month. Implement and follow a spending plan.

2. *Improve my fitness.* Design and follow a workout program to lower my body fat and improve my stamina. Eat nutritious, healthy meals on a regular schedule.

3. *Enjoy a more romantic relationship with my mate.* Plan a "date night" each week. Surprise him with loving gifts to let him know how much I care. Acknowledge him for all that he does and for all that he is.

This simple yet important step in designing your alliance will improve your understanding of how to best support each other. It will help you take action and stay focused on your most important goals.

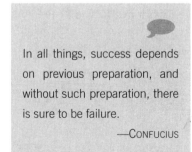

In all things, success depends on previous preparation, and without such preparation, there is sure to be failure.

—CONFUCIUS

Step 3: Prepare with a Success Partnership Form

It has been said that pale ink is better than the best memory. That is why a Success Partnership Form (SPF) can help you stay clear on what you said you would do, what you actually did, and what you plan on doing.

Each week, either fax or E-mail an SPF the day before you meet with your Success Partner. Whenever I sit down to fill out this form, it allows me to reflect on how effective I've been during the week and where I can improve. Clients have told me that preparing an SPF has been one of the best tools for enhancing their effectiveness and performance.

There are different sections to an SPF. The easiest way to use this form is to create a template, make copies of it, and fill one in every week. Following is a sample of a Success Partnership Form. Later you can customize the form to meet your needs.

SUCCESS PARTNERSHIP FORM

From: Joe Partner
Date: September 5
Meeting Time: 10:00 A.M.

CHECK IN (HOW WAS THE PAST WEEK?)

- Good. On a scale of 1 to 10 I'm feeling about an 8.

- The past week I was fairly focused and on track.

- I followed through on most of the agreements I made with myself and moved forward in many areas.

I WANT TO USE THIS PARTNERSHIP MEETING TO:

- Check in on what I did and what I plan to do.

- I also want to look at how I can stay focused on the projects that are most important right now, as opposed to working on the busy tasks that are not my priorities.

RESULTS OF MY GOALS FROM OUR LAST MEETING

- Finish the report for Mr. Jones [Yes].

- Invest at least two hours on the proposal for the Acme Company [Yes—three hours!].

- Go for a thirty-minute walk during lunch three times this week [No—did it twice].

- Go to the gym two times this week [Yes—three times!].

- Invest two hours going over family finances with my wife [Yes].

- Complete writing out my business goals for next year [No].

SUCCESSES AND WINS

- Wonderful trip to the lake with my family!

- Got the Smith account!

CHALLENGES AND OBSTACLES

- I focused on some busy tasks and did not get to all the main projects I wanted to work on.

MAJOR FOCUS AREAS IN MY LIFE THIS MONTH

- Completing the proposal for the Acme Company.

- Improving my health and fitness.

- Planning Jane's birthday party.

MY GOALS FOR THIS WEEK

- Invest at least two hours on the proposal for the Acme Company.

- Go for a thirty-minute walk during lunch three times.

- Go to the gym two times.

- Be in bed by 10:30 P.M. Sunday through Thursday night.

- Complete writing out my business goals for next year.

- Call three hotels for prices on Jane's birthday party.

As you can see, there are results from the past week and goals for the week to come. Preparing for your meetings with a Success Partnership Form can help you see what is working and where you might need to put some extra focus.

"The more you put into it, the more you get out of it." You've probably heard this before, and it definitely applies to getting the most out of a Success Partnership. The more effective you and your Success Partner are at supporting and empowering each other, the better results you both will get. There are four important lessons (or reminders) on how to be a great partner.

1. UNDERSTAND THE ART OF ACKNOWLEDGMENT

This is one of the greatest gifts you can give to each other. The present is most powerful when you recognize the special, personal qualities the person used to accomplish whatever action he took or awareness he achieved.

That was a major insight that Chris, who worked for one of the world's largest international management consulting businesses, had to learn. When he first came to me his main goal was to become a partner in his firm. Chris knew that in addition to putting in too many hours, he was poor at delegating and the people he managed were not performing well.

I asked Chris to list all his responsibilities. Then Chris figured out which ones he could delegate. He also set limitations on how many hours he would work, and he stuck to those boundaries.

Where Chris got bogged down was in his employees' performance. We discovered that he was not truly acknowledging people. Sure, he would say things like, "You did a good job on that report" or "Congratulations on making that sale," but he didn't truly identify their unique qualities that helped them in their accomplishments.

After Chris learned the art of acknowledgment, he started saying things like, "This report looks great. You are so good at paying attention to detail and meeting deadlines."

In time, Chris started to notice that his employees were better at following through on projects and taking more responsibility to boost their department as a whole. Basically, they thrived on his acknowledgment.

Practicing the art of acknowledgment did not only benefit Chris on the job; it also improved his personal life.

Chris was teaching his six-year-old daughter how to ride a bicycle by holding the back of her bicycle seat and running alongside her. After several tries, Chris said, "This time I'm going to let go for a little bit." Although she was afraid, his daughter agreed and she rode on her own for almost ten feet before she had to put her feet down to avoid falling.

Then Chris used his new art of acknowledgment as he praised, "You did great! I know it took a lot of courage for you to do that, and you didn't give up. I'm proud of you. You kept on going even though you were scared. You're a brave girl!"

Later that day, Chris's daughter came running inside and shouted, "Daddy, Daddy, come outside! I want to show you something!" He watched as his daughter pedaled all the way down their driveway, turned around, and came back again. Chris ran to his daughter and gave her a hug. She looked up at him with a big smile and said, "See, Daddy, I can do it now! I didn't quit even when I was scared!"

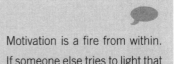

Motivation is a fire from within. If someone else tries to light that fire under you, chances are it will burn very briefly.

—STEPHEN R. COVEY, *THE 7 HABITS OF HIGHLY EFFECTIVE PEOPLE*

Acknowledgment is the articulation of your deep knowing of the other person. Look for what makes people great and let them know you see it. When you acknowledge your partner, remember to focus on him in addition to what he did. Highlight those distinctive, individual qualities he used in order to succeed.

Practice the art of acknowledgment and watch as your partner brings out more of his or her strengths and succeeds with greater ease.

2. MAKE SURE SHE REALLY WANTS A PUSH

One day our seven-year-old daughter Karina was playing on the swing set in our backyard. She swung back and forth slowly as she gazed down at her toes. I walked over and without asking gave a little push on her lower back. Annoyed, she chided me, "Papa, stop it! I don't want to swing high." Karina had been enjoying her leisurely, peaceful swing before I intruded.

How often do we push people without their consent? Permission is the simple act of asking, "Can I support you?" For some reason, many people think they have the duty and the right to go out and "fix" others. If you want to experience more empowering partnerships, you must be willing to trust that your partner's process may be different than yours. I've seen people cause problems in their partnerships because they tried to cheer up someone who needed to feel sad or pushed someone to get more done before they were ready.

That was the situation with David, an accountant I coached over two years. Forty-two years old, married with three young children, and the vice president of his firm, David was always on the move. He had big goals and he didn't let anything hold him back. He expected nothing less from others.

One day David told me that he had a "blowout" with a member of his staff. He had been demanding that a new accountant build her business by adding two new clients a week. Every time she didn't meet "her" goal, David would shake his head and tell her that she wasn't fully committed. Finally, she got fed up and confronted him.

"Why don't you focus on your own clients?" she snapped. "I'm far beyond what I planned to do this year, and whenever you tell me I'm not committed I feel like I'll never be able to enjoy my job!"

I asked David to think honestly about how he pressed his own value of high achievement on others. After a long silence David let out a soft sigh and admitted, "I never really looked at that." He had the "aha moment" that often occurs when we peer a little deeper into our own truth. He said that he was pressuring everyone, including his wife, children, brother, and the people at work. He realized that he had the distorted belief that it was his "job" to push people.

When David finally asked others how he could better support them, the most common response was "just ask me how things are going." David changed his style from pummeling to listening and in turn improved his relationships. Over time, he also gave himself more permission to enjoy his work—and his life—by going with the flow instead of always swimming against it.

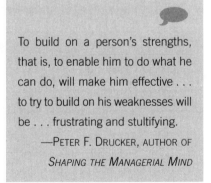

To build on a person's strengths, that is, to enable him to do what he can do, will make him effective . . . to try to build on his weaknesses will be . . . frustrating and stultifying.

—PETER F. DRUCKER, AUTHOR OF *SHAPING THE MANAGERIAL MIND*

3. REMEMBER, THE DEVIL DOESN'T NEED AN ADVOCATE

Several years ago I had a friend with whom I was reluctant to
share any of my ideas. It seemed that every time I told him
about something I wanted to do, he would have a reason why
it wasn't going to succeed. If it concerned business, he would
inform me about how it would fail. If I wanted to take a trip,
he would advise me about the dangers of travel or why the
destination was a poor choice. If I told him about someone I
was upset with, he would tell me all the reasons why that person was a jerk and declare, "Just don't talk to him."

This guy was a "devil's advocate," a person who examines
an idea by looking at the negative side of it. At the time, I
didn't have the courage to say, "Hey, why do you always
shoot my ideas down? I want your support, not your judgment." I don't know why he was always so negative when it
came to my desires. Maybe he was jealous and afraid that I
might become more successful than he was. Perhaps he
didn't want me to be happy or excited because he didn't feel
those ways. It really doesn't matter why. What matters is that
he taught me a crucial lesson by being the devil's advocate.

Have you ever had an idea and then a little voice in your
head starts to list all the reasons it won't work? We have our
own built-in devil's advocates, that negative inner voice that
tells us we can't succeed or that things are going to go wrong.
We don't need other people to join forces with our internal
devil's advocate.

My "friend" taught me that I'd rather be an angel's advocate, someone who would rather be encouraging and empa-
thetic, someone who would think about how it could
succeed instead of why it wouldn't.

Being an angel's advocate doesn't mean that you lie to
someone about your beliefs. It requires that first you listen,

ask questions, and focus on understanding what the person wants. Then if she asks you for your opinion, you can relate it without stomping on her idea.

The next time someone tells you his or her dream, first determine what you believe will work to fulfill it and then ask questions about the next steps. Be the angel's advocate.

4. ASK YOURSELF, "WHY AM I TALKING?"

There's an old saying in sales that goes, "You have two ears and one mouth; use them in that ratio." Many people don't realize that the easiest way to be a great conversationalist is by *not* talking. Have you ever heard people who seem to be reciting a monologue? They don't give you a chance to share your ideas or input as they go on and on about themselves. How do you feel when that happens?

When you talk, it is almost impossible to hear what the other person is really saying. This is a common cause of both relationship problems and lack of mutual support. If you just take the time to *really* listen, you will see a major improvement in your partnerships and your life. A simple way to remember this principle is the acronym WAIT, or

Why
Am
I
Talking?

In coaching and partnering, patient listening skills are fundamental. I have a little sign at my desk that says WAIT. When I coach (or meet with my Success Partner) and I find myself eager to give my opinion, I glance at it and I ask myself, Why am I preventing this person from tapping into his or her own wisdom? Am I so sure about being right and giving the answer to him? Am I uncomfortable about giving him the space to be silent if he chooses, which is often where the best answers are found?

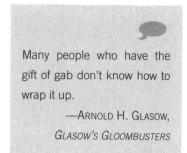

Many people who have the gift of gab don't know how to wrap it up.

—Arnold H. Glasow, *Glasow's Gloombusters*

If you want to better your relationships, your partnerships, and your life, remember to WAIT. You will be surprised at the learning and the benefit that you, and the person you are communicating with, will receive.

You're Ready to Reach New Heights

Now you have the strategies and the tools you need to form and maintain an effective Success Partnership. Use the power of partnership in your life and you'll be on the fast track to Extreme Success.

You'll see changes in just a week—if you set up your agreements and stick with them. I know people who have delayed their "to-do" list for years but once they joined with a Success Partner finally took action. They, too, achieved results in a week. But let's be realistic, too. Some changes are slower. However, they still happen, even if it takes several months. The point is to get going. Otherwise results are impossible.

Once in a while, a Success Partnership doesn't gel. There are signs: Maybe you're not looking forward to your meeting or you don't feel total support. Perhaps you were getting results, but they have stagnated. However, you may not have to start all over with someone new. Try redesigning your partnership. Go through the questions on page 121 with your partner again and determine what has changed for either of you. It may be that an extra boost of connection and trust is all you require to get both of you headed in the right direction once more.

Keepers: Thoughts to Remember

➤ Select a Success Partner whom you trust, can count on, and want to support, and who has a similar desire to do the same for you.

➤ Once you've chosen a Success Partner (and before your first meeting) suggest that he or she read the previous chapters in this book so that you're both on the same page.

➤ When you and your Success Partner decide to support each other's goals, a big step in designing your association will be your first meeting. There are four steps to be aware of for that meeting.

  1. Create Connection and Trust
  2. Clarify What You Want
  3. Prepare with a Success Partnership Form (SPF)
  4. Develop Your Partnership Skills

TO BE A GREAT SUCCESS PARTNER:

1. Understand the Art of Acknowledgment
2. Make Sure Your Success Partner Really Wants a Push
3. Remember, the Devil Doesn't Need an Advocate
4. Ask Yourself, "Why Am I Talking?"

Action Idea #12: Get Ready for a Success Partnership

Ask yourself the five questions (on pages 119–20) to see if you're ready for a Success Partnership. If so, then ask a friend, family member, or coworker. Schedule at least one hour for your initial meeting. Use the ten questions for your first meeting (on page 121) to design your partnership.

Action Idea #13: Clarify What You Want

Write down the three primary areas you would like to focus on during the first three months of your partnership. Ask your Success Partner to do the same and then make copies for each other.

For each focus area write a simple heading and underneath each a description of how to achieve it. See page 125 for an example.

9

An Alliance for Success

One finger can't lift a pebble.

—Hopi saying

For my first multi-pitch climb at Yosemite Valley I hired a guide who knew the territory inside and out. Walt had been a guide there for many years and he owned all the gear we would need for this exhilarating sport.

A multi-pitch is a climb where the route is higher than the length of a 200-foot rope. The leader ascends first while his belayer (in this case, me) lets out rope to him as he maneuvers up the cliff. When the leader gets to the end of the rope, he hooks himself in and then takes up the rope slack as his partner climbs. This process is repeated until both climbers arrive at the top of the cliff.

Walt taught me all the nuts and bolts of a big wall climb. He showed me how to manage the rope, place and remove the protective gear, and belay properly while hanging off a few spring-loaded devices called "cams" that we placed in various cracks in the rock on our way up the wall.

That day was a blast, thanks to Walt. Without the benefit

of his expertise it would have been a very slow, tiring, and unsafe attempt for me to navigate that route. I realized that hiring Walt was the smartest step I could have taken to advance me to the next level of climbing. Achieving a multi-pitch was a big goal of mine, and I understood that I couldn't have done it without him.

Many people become overwhelmed when they have a big goal. They believe that to reach their dream they need all types of resources that they lack. Often they shrug, give up, and declare, "I just don't have what it takes" or "I'll never be able to do all that."

I'm happy to say that outlook is all messed up. The truth is that other people can help you because they "have what it takes and they are able to do things"—and they are willing to make their special "gift" available to you. In fact, they are willing to form a special kind of partnership for that very purpose. It's called an alliance.

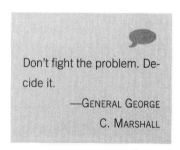

Don't fight the problem. Decide it.

—GENERAL GEORGE C. MARSHALL

There's More Than One Kind of Partner

In an Alliance Partnership, one person possesses something he or she shares with another person who requires it. This "something" might be experience, a specialized skill, contacts, or time and effort.

The giver receives something in return as well. It might be that keen sense of satisfaction that comes from lending a hand. It could be new business connections, help on tasks they don't want to do, or additional income, since they charge a fee for their services.

Do you see how Success Partnerships and Alliance Partnerships differ? In a Success Partnership, support and accountability are shared. In an Alliance Partnership, knowledge, skills, contacts, or time and effort might be exchanged. Here's another difference. It's best to have *one* Success Partner with whom you check in on a regular basis. You can have *many* Alliance Partners who aid you in all kinds of different ways.

Basically, an Alliance Partner helps you in ways that differ from a Success Partner. He or she can provide:

➤ leverage, a "leg up" that helps you do more than you can on your own;

➤ advice, which moves you faster and more easily toward your goals;

➤ connections, which allow you to meet people who can help you succeed.

One, two, or all three of these advantages can propel you on the path to Extreme Success a lot faster and with a lot less effort than if you try to accomplish everything on your own.

Arnold Schwarzenegger, for instance, has often been called a self-made man, but he's far from a solitary bodybuilder turned movie star and entrepreneur. People like Joe Gold, founder of Gold's Gym and World Gym, recognized Arnold's potential and introduced him to the "right" people. Joe Weider, publisher of the magazines *Muscle & Fitness* and *Shape* and founder of the Weider health product empire, was instrumental in making the name Schwarzenegger a household word. These

Alliance Partners helped build Arnold's amazing success. When Arnold hit the big time, he returned the favor by promoting Gold's and Weider's businesses through his image and reputation.

You don't have to be Mr. Universe to form an alliance but, like Arnold, you can benefit enormously from having one. For example, my client Amy, an accountant, wanted a Web site for her business. But since she and her husband were building a new house, she didn't have the funds to pay someone to design and build a Web site. We considered other possibilities and finally she decided to contact some Web masters and ask if they were interested in trading services.

Amy found John, who had recently left his dot-com job to start his own Web site creation and hosting company. It turned out that trying to do his own accounting left John feeling incompetent and overwhelmed.

Amy and John created an Alliance Partnership that helped each of them achieve what they wanted with less stress and strain and improved effectiveness. All they had to do was ask each other what they needed.

The Courage to Ask

The most common barrier I've seen when it comes to forming alliances is that people are reluctant to ask for support. They get stuck in the "I'll just handle it myself" mind-set and force themselves into performing overwhelming, frustrating, and low-quality work. Consequently, they don't attain success.

Asking for help is the mark of a person with confidence in her goals. She realizes what she needs to complete that objective. Consider the alliances we see every day in sports, in operating rooms, in space. All of the people involved in these high-achievement activities know their strengths—and one is the ability to ask for help when they need it.

Also, all of these people share their expertise to achieve success. Why should you be any different?

Right about now you may be thinking, But I don't have anything valuable to offer, so I shouldn't ask.

I bet you don't realize that you have something precious that could make a big difference in someone's life—a person who, in turn, could aid you in your quest for success.

Here's the deal. *You must take the risk of asking.* That way you set the stage for getting the information required to form an alliance through clarity and communication. It's the only way you will discover how you might be able to give—and receive—assistance now and in the future.

When you approach someone to be in alliance with you, all you need to say is, "Is there any way that I might be able to help you?" The openness and relief that others show may surprise you. After all, just about everyone is looking for a boost, only you can't see it. They will likely be very happy to tell you more than one way you could fulfill a task for them that they can't carry out for themselves.

So don't buy into the fiction that you have nothing to offer. Just asking shows that you want to reciprocate a favor. The person on the receiving end will be so glad to know it.

Break the Ice

There's another barrier that prevents people from inviting someone to be their Alliance Partner. They think they have to get everything "ready" first.

That's what my client Jeff, who had been working at a

commercial real estate company for less than a year, thought. He told me, "This company has offices in five states. My goal is to be in the top ten percent of all of the brokers in the firm within three years."

This seemed like a clear aim until I asked, "How will you know when you get there?"

Jeff had no idea.

Then I said, "Who is the most successful broker in your company?" Again, he didn't know, and so finding out became his assignment.

A week later Jeff told me he discovered that one of the top people worked at his office! Knowing that successful people often will help out newcomers, I suggested that he ask this woman if she would be willing to share some tips on how he could move toward the top.

"I don't think I'm totally prepared to ask her that yet," Jeff replied.

"What do you mean?"

"Well, I want to build up my numbers first and get some more experience so I don't look like such a novice."

Clearly, Jeff was stuck in preparation mode.

"I challenge you, as a new broker, to request one tip from her. Will you do that?"

"Okay," he conceded. "It's probably the best thing I could do right now because I'm not really sure what my next step is."

The following week a very different Jeff related how he had asked for advice and informed the established broker about his objective. Sensing his desire and commitment, she threw him an unexpected, although very welcome, curve.

It seemed that she was in the process of reducing her client load because she wanted to specialize in real estate for those in the medical field. She offered Jeff an alliance right then and there. He would take on the clients she was giving up, and he would pass on to her a percentage of those commissions. It was a win-win for both of them.

At last Jeff realized that waiting until he felt "totally prepared" didn't make sense. Because he had the courage to act when he did, he seized an opportunity that he established for himself. (Not to mention the fact that he "created" his own luck.) Here's the thing to remember about Alliance Partnerships:

If you think you don't have something valuable to offer another person, you will struggle.

When you offer your experience and skill to someone else in exchange for something he or she

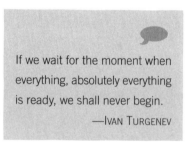

If we wait for the moment when everything, absolutely everything is ready, we shall never begin.
—IVAN TURGENEV

has to offer, you create an alliance that satisfies you both—and creates success with greater ease.

Giver's Gain

A lot of successful people believe that because someone aided them in the past it is their duty to do the same for others now and in the future. In cases like these, an Alliance Partner wants nothing in return. The reward is the warm feeling he or she gets from offering assistance.

For example, my client Tim wanted to learn more about what it really takes to open a Starbucks franchise. He asked the owner of a successful Starbucks if he could interview her for half an hour. She said she would be honored to share her knowledge. She even referred Tim to two other Starbucks

owners who ran profitable businesses. Tim learned the price-
less secrets of three experienced "masters" just by asking.

I've found that most people are glad to lend a hand as long
as it doesn't severely infringe on their time or impact nega-
tively on their reputation in some way.

Remember: Even if you don't think you have something
to offer the person you are asking, don't let that put you off.
Likely your assets will fulfill someone else's need down the
road. It's kind of a karma thing. What comes around goes
around.

Build on a Strong Foundation

Relationship building is a major part of creating successful alliances. I vividly remember driving with my friend Brandon
to go skiing near Lake Tahoe. It was mid-January and we
were talking about the previous year's successes, wins, challenges, and lessons.

I told Brandon, "My biggest lesson last year was how important relationships are to my success. A lot of people
helped me out so that I could reach my goals. There's no way
I'd be where I am without the help they gave me. Relationships are key."

Brandon thought about my lesson. Then he said, "Yeah,
and I think it's more than just relationships. It's about *quality*
relationships. Rich, if you hadn't established trust, connection, and friendship with those people, they wouldn't have
helped you as much as they did."

Brandon made an insightful point. In order to have the desire to help you, people have to feel that you're trustworthy.
We all know that it's human nature to watch people and then

talk about them. I've seen again and again that when people form an impression, either positive or negative, about someone, that becomes the filter through which they observe that person. They will seek evidence to confirm their beliefs. If they view you as a giver, they will search for all the generous things you do. If they view you as a taker, they will hunt for all the things you grab.

Make no mistake. Opinions are formed by your actions, which demonstrate who you are. This is a major factor in determining whether someone is willing to create an Alliance Partnership with you.

Many of my Alliance Partners began as friends. I was first attracted to the people who have assisted me because of their authenticity and because they enjoy the two-way support that a quality friendship can give. I discovered that people who live this way want to help one another however they can.

You attract people who operate the way you do. That's why, to present yourself as a quality Alliance Partner, you must act like one.

A Little Money Goes a Long Way

If you want to leap from surviving to thriving and can't find someone to create an alliance with, then get out there and hire someone! The exchange is straightforward. You pay for experience, specialized skill, contacts, or efforts.

When I wanted to bring my ideas to the world through my writing I didn't sit in my office trying to do it all on my own. I knew there were very talented and experienced people out there who could make the process a whole lot easier and more enjoyable.

First, I met with a person who specializes in helping consultants, coaches, and speakers discover and simplify their particular messages and techniques. Then I hired a professional writer and editor to get my unique message and strategies into a top-notch book proposal. Next I found an agent to place my polished proposal into the hands of the best publishers. Then, when several publishers asked me to fly to New York for interviews, I hired a media coach who prepared me by clarifying what I wanted to say and how I wanted to say it. And finally, I found a great publisher who provided me with an incredible editor along with a dynamite publicity and sales team.

You see, I didn't leave anything to chance. I also didn't try to struggle on my own to achieve the outcome I wanted. I gained the support, talent, experience, and the energy of a whole team of people who partnered with me to achieve my goal.

All these folks gained from their alliance with me as well. Referrals of new clients, word-of-mouth praise, greater income, and a new perspective on success were the benefits I helped provide to them.

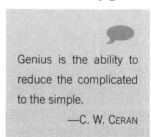

Genius is the ability to reduce the complicated to the simple.

—C. W. CERAN

Keepers: Thoughts to Remember

ALLIANCE PARTNERSHIPS PROVIDE:

_____ leverage, which helps you do more than you can on your own;

_____ advice, which moves you faster and more easily toward your goals;

_____ connections, which allow you to meet people who can help you succeed.

➤ In an Alliance Partnership, one person possesses something he or she shares with another person who requires it. This "something" might be experience, a specialized skill, contacts, or time and effort.

➤ If you think you don't have something valuable to offer to another person, you will struggle.

➤ When you offer your experience and skill to someone else in exchange for something he or she has to offer, you create an alliance that satisfies you both.

➤ A common barrier to forming alliances is the reluctance to ask for support. _You must take the risk of asking._

➤ Relationship building is a major part of creating successful alliances.

➤ If you can't find someone to create an alliance with, then you can hire the right person for your needs. You can pay for experience, specialized skill, contacts, or efforts.

Action Idea #14: Know the Value of Alliances

This exercise can show you how an alliance can work. Just think how mentors and associates have given you information, training, feedback, support, or connections. Jot down the names of three mentors, teachers, or specialists who have helped you to be more successful.

1. _____

2. _____

3. _____

Now write down how they did it.

1. _____

2. _____

3. _____

Great! Now you're more prepared to ask someone else to be an Alliance Partner, because you have a better idea of what has worked well for you in the past.

Action Idea #15: Get Ready to Form an Alliance

What is one thing you have been putting off because you believe that you lack the experience, contacts, abilities, or time to make an Alliance Partnership happen?

_____

Name three ways that you might be able to use an Alliance Partner to help you achieve that goal.

1. _____

2. _____

3. _____

What is the next step you will take to use an Alliance Partner for your success?

_____

PART 4

Watch Where You're Going

10

Check Out That View

The clearer you are about what you want, and what you are willing to do to get it, the more likely it is that you will be lucky and get what you want. Clarity of desired goals is a magnet that draws good luck to you.

—Brian Tracy, author and speaker

Years ago my grandparents owned a little cabin in New Hampshire. Every summer our family would go there for vacation. One of the best parts of staying there was the nearby lake.

One day my older brother Rob said, "Hey, Rich, you're old enough to swim to the island on the far side of the lake. Wanna do it?"

I still remember the fears that rushed through my mind at that moment. I thought I'd either need an emergency rescue team to save me from drowning or, worse, from a giant snapper turtle swimming up from the depths to pull me under for his late-afternoon snack.

At thirteen, Rob had already made the swim, along with our dad, to the island each of the past four years. I was nine years old and I knew it was time for me to accept the challenge. It was just that brotherly thing to do.

Rob and I stood at the edge of the lake and looked far across the water. The island seemed miles away. Privately, I was having a hard time believing that I could make the swim. I was relieved when my dad walked over and said, "I'll row beside you boys in the boat, just in case."

Rob and I dove in and began to swim. About halfway across the lake I was exhausted. Rob was already about fifty feet in front of me and didn't seem tired at all. I wanted to make it to the island so badly, but my body weighed me down like an anchor.

"Rob, how come I'm so tired?" I yelled out.

"Because you're swimming in a zigzag!" he shouted back. "You gotta keep looking up to make sure you're heading toward the island!"

It worked! I learned that all I had to do was frequently glance at my destination. This kept me from veering off course and putting in a lot more strokes. Thanks to Rob's advice, I made it all the way to the island—and started to enjoy myself along the way. (Thanks to my dad, I got a ride back in the rowboat.)

Later that evening, when we were having dinner, I turned to my little brother Steve and said, "When you're big enough I'll show *you* how to swim to the island."

Focus Is Not an Effort

That day I learned something very interesting. I already knew that there was nothing wrong with making an effort. After all, I was ready and willing to head to the island. I accepted Rob's challenge and I wanted to accomplish something I had never done before. What I learned along the way was something new and different. I found out that the only thing wrong with effort was if I wasted it and struggled. I discovered focused effort, that is, concentrating on where I wanted to go in an effective way that gave me enjoyment on the way to my goal.

Sadly, this is not the way most people operate when a big job looms ahead. What I most often hear is, "I need to really put in some hard work" or something to that effect. When they say this, all they do is set themselves up for more work—and struggle.

When a person focuses his energy and thoughts on the "I must work hard" mantra, he often ends up laboring against fear, procrastination, lack of clarity, and mistakes. This happens for a simple reason: Because he isn't clear on his goal, he zigzags (like I did), which ends up exhausting him and moving him further from his intention.

Here's the hard truth: Hard work doesn't guarantee great results.

In contrast, when you use *focused effort*, you apply your drive toward the result you want to achieve. Your energy is not scattered all over, with you running in circles. With focused effort, you can achieve your desired result smoothly and with greater ease.

But before you can focus your effort you must know one thing: what your goal is.

You Have to Know Where You're Going in Order to Get There

CHANDLER: "Hey, you guys in the living room all know what you want to do. You know, you have goals. You have dreams. I don't have a dream.
ROSS: Ah, the lesser known "I Don't Have a Dream" speech.

—from the TV sitcom *Friends*

If you've ever felt like Chandler, you are not alone. Many people tell me they lack an intention, a vision of their future, and this keeps them from achieving Extreme Success.

If you're not sure of what you want your outcome to be, you're setting yourself up for a tough time. Whether it's performing a sport, writing a song, creating a business plan, or deciding on where you want to vacation, gaining clarity on what you want to achieve for a future outcome is vital.

A vision is simply a very clear picture of what you see for yourself in the future if everything turns out just right. A powerful, compelling vision is exciting and magnetic. But most important, a clear vision provides you with direction and imparts meaning to your work and life.

I believe that forming a vision honors your priorities. That's because priorities ensure that you accomplish what is most important—as opposed to what appears to be most urgent. That's why concentrating on your priorities helps you determine what needs to happen for you to realize the goals you value most.

If you don't concentrate your energy this way, something will happen that you may not like. It may have happened already. If you don't have a future intention for your life, you might find yourself working for someone who does. That's

> What I am most happy about is that I can zero in on a vision of where I want to be in the future. I can see it so clearly in front of me when I daydream that it's almost reality. Then I get this easy feeling, and I don't have to be uptight because I already feel like I'm there, that it's just a matter of time.
>
> —ARNOLD SCHWARZENEGGER

why if you want to achieve Extreme Success, you must clarify what it means for *you*. I believe that Extreme Success is reaching the goals you've set for yourself and living your own way. It's being the person that you want to be.

When you aren't clear on your goal, your chances of achieving it lessen and, as a result, you struggle.

When you get clear on your intention, you target your thoughts and energy on achieving your goal with effectiveness, momentum, and satisfaction.

Look to the Future for Your Next Steps Today

Think of what it's like to peer through a zoom lens. At first everything is hazy and unclear. When you aim the camera on a specific object and adjust the lens, however, the object begins to appear sharper. As you focus the lens some more, everything else in the viewfinder blurs slightly. And while you know other objects are there, they don't distract you. You can also see other opportunities that might appear, but you don't have to lose clear sight of your original intention unless you choose to adjust your focus.

In life, getting clear on what you are moving toward helps you see what your next steps need to be. You can concentrate your energy on what really matters most instead of wavering around without a desired outcome.

That's the power of directing your attention on your intention.

By now you may be saying, Okay, Rich, I know I need to define my intention. But if I don't know what it is, what can I do?

First, I suggest that you imagine how you want your life to be in one year and then write out that vision. Use the categories from the Life Balance Wheel (see page 54) and describe how you want that area of your life at that future date.

Another method that can aid you in creating a compelling vision is to define what you don't want. Many people warn, "If you focus on what you don't want, you will attract more of it." I suggest going beyond that belief. I say shed light on what you don't like. Put it out on the table and check it out. Then flip it over. What's on the other side?

For example, if you say, "I don't want to do the same type of monotonous work day in and day out," turn it over. The opposite may be something like, "I want my job to be creative and change over time. I want to make the most of my imaginative mind because I crave variety in my work."

Imagining and visualizing can also assist you in creating your plans and help you see how to prepare for possible future opportunities. It is also one of the most important factors in *seeing* an opportunity present itself. That way you are more likely to be in the right place at the right time.

One exercise I've seen deliver incredible results for my clients is called Future Focus. It's based on the principle that all things are created twice, first in the mind and then in a physical form. If you begin by visualizing what you want, you can then produce it with more clarity and purpose.

The Future Focus exercise taps into your imagination to help you illuminate what you want to be, do, and have in the future. You'll actually experience meeting and sharing a day with your Future Self and see the vision of your future. Your Future Self can be a powerful resource, a mentor, and an adviser to guide you toward being the person that you want to become. I suggest using this visualization regularly—once a month. Over time, you'll discover a new sense of courage, confidence, and clarity.

To get the most value from Future Focus, I suggest that you record yourself reading it and then play it back as you listen with your eyes closed. When you're ready to do the exercise, find a comfortable place where you won't be interrupted for at least ten minutes. If you have visualized or meditated before, get into the position that works best for you. If you have not, I suggest sitting upright in a comfortable chair with your feet flat on the floor and your hands in your lap.

Allow yourself to relax fully and begin focusing on your breathing. Breathe in through your nose and hold it for a moment. Then breathe out through your mouth. Allow yourself to be conscious of your easy, natural, and effortless breathing. Let each breath make you more relaxed and comfortable. Let any tension leave your body. Relax your neck and shoulders and move your head gently from side to side a few times.

Thoughts may pass through your mind. Think of them as white clouds floating overhead and let them slowly drift by. Allow yourself to feel calm, content, relaxed, and peaceful. Continue to focus on your breathing as you slowly contract all the muscles in your body from your feet to your head. Curl your toes, tighten your legs, clench your fists, bring your shoulders up toward your ears, tighten up your jaw and then your forehead, take a deep breath in, hold it, and, as you exhale, allow your entire body to relax completely. Feel how wonderful it is.

Now imagine that you are walking along a winding path. Notice the environment. Are there trees? Flowers? What color is the sky? As you continue walking look up ahead. You see a huge door. Really notice what this door looks like. See its color and texture. As you approach this door, understand that it is magical. On the other side is your future where you will have the opportunity to see where you will be and what your life will look like at any time in your future.

You have the opportunity to choose how far into your future you wish to travel. You may want to see where you will be in one year, or maybe five, ten, or even twenty years hence. Decide now how many years into the future you would like to journey.

Notice that you still feel calm, content, relaxed, and peaceful. After you have chosen the future you would like to see, take a deep breath and place your hand on the door. Now slowly push the door open and step through to the other side. You are now standing in the year you have chosen to visit. As you look ahead, you see a dwelling. This is where your Future Self lives.

As you approach the home of your Future Self, notice what it looks like. Glance around. Really get a sense of this place. You are welcome here. Now walk to the door of your Future Self's home.

As you look closer, notice that the door is slightly open. Step through the doorway and into this dwelling. Observe the inside. What kind of person lives here? What are the colors of this place?

Now, say hello and listen. Hear the voice of your Future Self reply from the other room. It is you in the future you have chosen to see. Your Future Self is coming to meet you. Watch your Future Self enter the room.

Greet your Future Self and pay attention to the way your Future Self welcomes you to this time and place. Study what your Future Self looks like. What is your Future Self wearing? How does your Future Self stand? Really get a sense of the type of person. Feel how good it is to be here.

Your Future Self invites you to share some time together.

You will have the opportunity to see the life of your Future Self. You'll see the kind of person your Future Self is and what your Future Self does.

There are questions you might want to ask. Begin with the following: "What would be most helpful for me to know to get to where you are?" Listen to what your Future Self tells you.

After your Future Self answers, it is a good time to pose your own questions. What would you like to ask your Future Self?

Enjoy this time with your Future Self and know that throughout this visit, you can ask your Future Self whatever questions you may have.

Follow your Future Self through the day. What is your Future Self doing? Where does your Future Self go?

As you follow your Future Self through the day, observe the different life areas and notice the achievements. What are the relationships like? Who are the most important people in your Future Self's life?

What about the health and fitness of your Future Self? Take note of physical condition and vitality.

Ask your Future Self the following question: "In your day, what is the most important thing that you do?" Listen to what your Future Self tells you.

Now that you have spent most of the day with your Future Self, you may have some other questions about areas of your Future Self's life that you want to know more about. What other questions would you like to ask your Future Self?

It's time to leave. Before you do, ask your Future Self this final question: "What other advice do you have for me before I go?" Listen to what your Future Self tells you.

Thank your Future Self for the wisdom and for sharing this day with you. Whenever you need guidance, courage, or wisdom, you can visit your Future Self. Know that your Future Self will always be a powerful resource for you.

Say good-bye understanding that you will remember everything you need to from this visit. Notice the way your Future Self returns your farewell.

Now find your way back to the door that led you into this future. On the other side is the date you arrived from. As you step toward the door, notice that you feel calm, content, relaxed, and peaceful.

Take a deep breath and place your hand on the door. Slowly push the door open and step through to the other side. Observe that you are again walking on the path and you are back to the time you left from. As you continue walking along the path realize that you are back in the present and that you have returned to the room from which you originally left.

Slowly take a deep breath and then exhale. Feel yourself back in the room. Be conscious of becoming more alert and notice how refreshed you feel. Take another deep breath and then exhale. Become aware of your body and your breathing. Stretch your body, feeling the ground beneath you. Take one more breath and exhale. Before you move, be aware of the inner peace, confidence, and joy that you are feeling.

Write down the answers to these questions after you do the Future Focus exercise:

1. Where were you and what did it look like?
2. How did your Future Self greet you?
3. What did your Future Self look like?
4. What kind of person is your Future Self?
5. What questions did your ask your Future Self?

6. What did your Future Self say when you asked the question "What would be most helpful for me to know to get to where you are?"
7. What did your Future Self say when you asked the question "In your day, what is the most important thing that you do?"
8. What other advice or information did your Future Self offer you?
9. What surprised you about what you saw?

Seeing Is Believing

Shane, a thirty-year-old salesperson for a business-to-business software company, was very happy with his finances and his marriage. He hired me to coach him because he was frustrated with the rest of his life. Nothing else rated above a 5 on his Life Balance Wheel. The fun and recreation area was the lowest with a rating of 1. When I've seen this in the past it's typical to see a much higher work satisfaction level. Many people put such a focus on being successful at work that time to play suffers. But Shane rated his career as a 2.

When I asked him about his low ratings he told me, "I just feel like I'm running on empty. Every time I call a prospective company, something inside of me hopes they will say no. I feel overloaded, so I'm trying to avoid any more work. I want to just give it all up and move to a cabin in the mountains. Something has to change."

I asked Shane how he envisioned his life in ten years. "Pretty much the same," he replied. I realized that he and I needed to have a better idea of where he wanted to be instead of where he thought he had to be. So we did the Future Focus exercise together.

Shane loved his Future Self. He described him as a peaceful and confident man with lots of passion. Shane said his Future Self was still with the same company but had a completely different style of working. He had a whole team supporting him and he worked only six hours a day (about half of what Shane had been working). Shane went on to describe his Future Self as grounded, handsome, and full of vitality.

He also had a much better relationship with God. Shane had prayed every day from early childhood through college and went to church every day. When he got out into the working world, however, his religion was the first thing he abandoned. Now Shane was realizing its importance for his own peace of mind and fulfillment.

When he was visualizing his Future Self, Shane asked him, "What do I need to do to get from where I am to where you are?" His Future Self told him to get back to church and start praying again. He also told him that he needed to get help and stop working so many hours. Finally, his Future Self suggested that Shane start playing tennis again, the way he had in college.

Shane took his Future Self's advice. In less than two weeks he had hired an administrative assistant to handle his detail work. He stopped wasting time on cold calls by hiring someone to phone prospective clients and screen them to see if they wanted Shane to follow up with them.

He also made a commitment with his wife to be home every day by six o'clock, and he signed up for a tennis league that met two nights a week. Finally, Shane renewed his commitment to his religion and started going to church once a week as well as taking time for daily prayer.

By listening to the wisdom of his Future Self (which was really tapping into Shane's inner truth) Shane dramatically improved his life, both personally and professionally. He was working less, earning more, and felt a new sense of calm. When he filled out a Life Balance Wheel three months later, every area of Shane's life was at level 7 or above.

After Shane had worked with me for about a year and a half, I gave him a question to think about for a week. I asked him to ponder, "How have you become more like your Future Self?"

At our next coaching session, Shane said, "I gave a lot of thought to that inquiry. The truth is that I have already *become* my Future Self. When we did the exercise, I saw that guy ten years out. But now I can see that I'm living the way that he was in that visualization. I feel like I'm really walking my talk. Before, I thought that things couldn't change. Now I realize that it was *me* who had to change first."

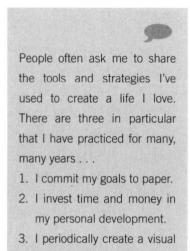

People often ask me to share the tools and strategies I've used to create a life I love. There are three in particular that I have practiced for many, many years . . .

1. I commit my goals to paper.
2. I invest time and money in my personal development.
3. I periodically create a visual map of my desires.

—CHERYL RICHARDSON,
LIFE MAKEOVERS

Create the Picture of Your Dreams

When I was a little boy, a couple of months before Christmas, my mom would ask my brothers and me to make "wish list posters." We would go through catalogs and magazines and cut out pictures of special toys and gadgets that we wanted for presents. Then we would paste them onto a big poster board and make a collage. We always loved this tradition and it got us extra excited for the upcoming holiday. Little did my mom know that she was showing us the basics of creating a Dream Gallery.

A Dream Gallery is a poster or a three-ring binder that displays images and words of the things you want to have in your life, such as experiences, people, material possessions, and feelings. These images often display values like freedom, play, romance, achievement, or beauty. They also can represent personal qualities you want to develop such as calmness, courage, or an open mind. Basically, a Dream Gallery is a visual reminder of images and words that inspire you and remind you of your dreams.

My mom may have introduced the idea of a Dream Gallery to me thirty years ago, but since then I've also heard it called a treasure map, dream board, vision poster, and more. It doesn't really matter what you call it. As you can imagine, there are no limits to the creativity you can put into this. I know someone who created a personal Web site for her Dream Gallery.

In my workshops I have watched people go through the process of creating their own Dream Galleries, and one thing is always the same: They always have a blast doing it and derive many benefits from the process.

Creating a Dream Gallery is also a great activity to do with your Success Partner or with a group of friends. It's not only a fun project, it also gets you to really think about what you want in your life. By seeking images and words that inspire you, you'll discover what you long for on a deeper level. Taking the time to assemble a Dream Gallery gives your head and your heart a way to say, "Here is what we really want." As the sculpture on my desk says: KEEP YOUR HEAD AND YOUR HEART IN THE RIGHT DIRECTION AND YOU'LL NEVER HAVE TO WORRY ABOUT YOUR FEET.

Looking at your Dream Gallery gives you extra motivation while putting you in a terrific mood. By including pictures of what you already possess, such as family, friends, a home, a car, hobbies, and/or fitness, you will remind yourself to be grateful and appreciate what you have. By adding pictures and words that focus on what you want, you will better clarify what you are working toward by inspiring yourself on a regular basis. It's like high-octane motivation fuel.

Tell Yourself What You Really, Really Want

When I was in my early twenties I kept dreaming of how I wanted my life to be. Every time I read a story about someone successful, noticed someone living his or her dreams, or saw a house or car I really loved, I'd take a mental note and put it in my mind's "dream bank."

One day I was tape-recording notes for my college homework and I started to daydream. I saw myself in my ideal future, really getting the most out of life. The image was so clear that I had to capture it. I pushed record, closed my eyes, and began to describe a day in my ideal future.

I ended up with an inspiring tape that I played on a regular basis whenever I needed an extra recharge of motivation to achieve my dreams. I didn't know it then, but I had actually come up with an exercise for my first audiotape program that I produced ten years later entitled *FOCUS: A Guide to Clarity and Achievement*.

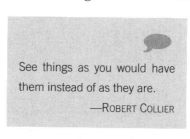

See things as you would have them instead of as they are.

—ROBERT COLLIER

You can easily create your own Audio Vision by doing the

Future Focus exercise, taking mental notes, and then recording your voice as you describe a day in your ideal future. Have fun!

The Rule of Three

Another strategy that can help you stay focused on your main intention and at the same time help you avoid being overwhelmed is the Rule of Three. That is, holding your focus on no more than three major intentions at the same time. This rule applies to both your long-term and day-to-day intentions.

Yeah, Rich, you might be saying, but I have so many things I want or need. How am I supposed to limit my focus to three things?

I understand. But consider that every day you are bombarded with hundreds of tasks, messages, and people competing for your attention and time. The bottom line is if you try to "hold" too much in your mind, everything becomes vague and confusing. I'm not saying to try to limit your life to only three things. You can keep your other goals organized on paper, but it's important to have no more than three major intentions that you keep very present in your mind and in front of you. When you focus this way, your mind can retain and process them with greater clarity. Diffused focus is no focus at all.

That's why I recommend using what I call the "reverse funnel effect." Think of your intentions this way.

At the narrowest part are your three main intentions for the day. A little up from that come your three main intentions for the week. Further up are your three main intentions for the month. As the funnel widens more there are your three main intentions for the year. The big intention—the goal you see in your Future Focus or Dream Gallery or Audio Vision—is the widest part of the funnel. Everything you do feeds into the big intention, but by breaking the components into smaller-sized bits they are more manageable, which means you won't struggle when you do them.

If I asked you, "What are your three main intentions this month?" you should be able to answer me without hesitation. This is the key to the Rule of Three. Your intentions are so clear and present in your mind that you are aware of all opportunities that can move you toward achieving them faster and with greater ease. By using the Rule of Three, you will also greatly increase your intentional luck because you will have a strategy, you will be prepared, and you will see many more opportunities when they arrive.

Here's how to do it. As soon as you have a solid idea of what you wish to achieve and what you want your life to "look like" in the future, write down three major goals you would like to accomplish this year that will move you toward your long-term vision. These are your three main intentions. (Read them at least once a week to make sure you are heading in the right direction. Like me swimming toward the island, periodically you must pick your head up and check out where your efforts are taking you. This will focus your effort rather than waste it.)

The next step is to look at your yearly intentions at the beginning of every month and create one monthly intention for each. Write them down and keep them visible. For example, if your goal is to buy a new house by year's end, you may need to save a certain amount of money by the end of the month. If another intention is to lose twenty pounds by December 31, you may want to lose four more pounds by month's end. You get the idea.

Next, describe in writing the three intentions for the coming week that will help create the monthly intentions. Put them where you can see them.

Finally, bring the Rule of Three into your daily living by defining and writing down which three intentions that day will support your three intentions for the week. Make sure these are visible, too. (I've had clients who E-mailed me their three intentions for the day. The next morning they gave me a report on how they did and then told me the three intentions for that day.)

The Rule of Three is a powerful strategy to use in your Success Partnership as well. Each month share your three main intentions with your Success Partner. If you meet weekly, share what your three main intentions are for the coming week.

Knowing how you want to live in the present moment and then living that way allows the future to take care of itself.

Keepers: Thoughts to Remember

➤ If you focus your energy on thinking, I must work hard, you end up struggling against fear, procrastination, confusion, and mistakes.

➤ If you get clear on your intention, you can use *focused effort* to apply your drive toward the result you *want* to achieve.

➤ To succeed, you must have a vision, a clear picture of what you see for yourself in the future if things turn out just right.

➤ One way to help yourself create a compelling vision is to identify what you *don't* want. Imagination and visualization can help you see what you *do* want.

➤ For maximum results, use the Rule of Three: Focus on no more than three major intentions at the same time.

➤ If you keep intentions clear and present in your mind, you will become aware of opportunities that can move you toward achieving them faster and with greater ease.

➤ If you know how you want to live in the present, the future will take care of itself.

Action Idea #16: Meet Your Future Self

Record yourself reading the Future Focus script on pages 159–62. Then play it back as you listen with your eyes closed. This exercise will tap into your imagination to help you illuminate what you want to be, do, and have in the future.

Your Future Self can be a powerful resource, a mentor, and an adviser to guide you toward being the person that you want to become.

NOTE: Rich Fettke narrates the Future Focus exercise on the audiotape and compact disc version of *Extreme Success* (available from Simon & Schuster Audio).

Action Idea #17: Create a Dream Gallery

Get a stack of magazines and cut out the images and words that best express how you see your ideal future. Then arrange and paste those images and words on a poster board or in a three-ring binder so it displays the experiences and the things that you want to have in your life.

Your Dream Gallery will inspire you to take action and stay focused on what is most important so you can move toward it with less distraction. It will also help you hold clear images in your mind of what you want in your life, which will increase your awareness of opportunities.

Action Idea #18: Create an Audio Vision

Complete the Future Focus exercise in Action Idea #16. Take mental notes and then make another recording. This time, record your voice as you describe a day in your ideal future. Vividly describe what happens from the time you wake up until the time you go to bed.

You will then have an inspiring recording that you can play on a regular basis whenever you want an extra recharge of motivation.

Action Idea #19: Use the Rule of Three

Use the Rule of Three and identify your three main intentions for the coming year. From those intentions, you can clarify your three main intentions for the month, the week, and your days. Remember: Your Success Partner can be a powerful support in making the most of this strategy by reminding you of your intentions and by holding you accountable to making progress on them.

When you are beginning your partnership write out and share your three main intentions for the coming year. Then, each month, write out and share your three main intentions for the coming month (these will most likely support your yearly intentions). Then each week share your three main intentions for the coming week. When you begin each day (or the night before) clarify the three main outcomes you want to achieve that day (these will most likely support your weekly intentions).

11

Hocus Focus

Let your hook be always cast. In the pool where you least expect it, will be fish.

—Ovid

I leaned hard to the left as I followed Rob down the single-track mountain bike trail at teeth-chattering speed. I was concentrating hard on his back tire as it spewed rocks and dirt when all of a sudden he launched into the air off a big, flat rock sticking out of the downhill slope.

Then it happened. I was flying over a rocky landing as my bike and body became weightless. I didn't have a nanosecond to think as my front tire dug into the ground. Then I felt my torso speeding forward while my hands kept a death grip on the handlebars.

The next thing I remember was lying flat on my back and staring up at Rob. "Dude, are you okay?" he asked with concern as he leaned over me.

"Yeah. What happened?" I muttered as I sat up, dazed.

"I'm not sure. I only heard you crash. I think you went OTB."

"What's OTB?"

Rob gestured at my twisted bike about ten feet up the hill and answered, "Over the bars, man. Over the bars."

No wonder. I had mentally checked out, placing all my attention on one small detail of our trip. All I was concerned with was keeping up with Rob; that's why I kept my eyes on his back tire. Big mistake. I should have maintained a wide focus on where we were heading.

This lesson was a great reminder that I needed to stay clear on where I intended to go and not lose awareness by concentrating on only one aspect of the journey. That path threw me a surprise when I wasn't ready.

That's not to say that Rob and I didn't prepare beforehand. We did. We knew where we wanted to go and we had the right equipment. But when we arrived at the top of the hill, I should have realized there were many different ways to get to the bottom.

Right about now you may be thinking, Gee, Rich, you and Rob should have had a plan for the ride. Then, maybe, you wouldn't have gotten wrecked.

Nice thought, but that wasn't the problem. We could see far down into the valley (our desired outcome or ending point) and we could see what was in front of us (the next few turns, rocks, drop-offs, etc.). But it was impossible to figure out the *exact* turns by trying to come up with a detailed plan. If we did that, eventually the sun would have set and our chance for a fun ride would have slipped away with it.

Instead, to make the most of the ride, it would have made sense (and been a lot less painful) to remember that our intention was to arrive at the bottom of the valley and enjoy the journey.

Had I kept that awareness in mind—*while keeping a wide focus about where I was going, a few turns at a time*—I would have anticipated both the opportunities and hazards that cropped up as we sped down the hill. In due course I would have reached our goal with a lot of joy along the way— and without an unplanned detour over the handlebars of my bike.

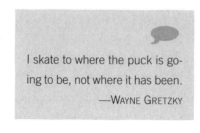

I skate to where the puck is going to be, not where it has been.
—WAYNE GRETZKY

A Wide-angle Focus = A Big, Clear Picture

I've noticed that after people get clear on their vision and goals, many of them shift into microfocus. They believe there is only one way of doing things and just one single-lane path to their desired outcome. As a result they trap themselves in "analysis paralysis" by focusing too hard on one aspect of reaching their intention. When this happens it's like they put on binders, which let them see only what is directly in front of them. (That's what happened to me and I paid for it. Struggle, anyone?) Of course, it also means that not only are the perils ahead out of their line of vision, so are the tremendous opportunities. Worst of all, they lose sight of where they truly want to go.

That's why you shouldn't buy into that old line of thinking, Make a plan and then work the plan. It just doesn't hold true anymore. There are too many variables in the marketplace now. Prospects can pop up in an instant and zip by just as fast.

That's why results do not come from detailed planning!

For example, a football team has one intention: to win. And while it has a plan for that goal, the team must—and does—change plays during the game because of variables it could not have anticipated, like weather, injury, or the opposing quarterback making the play of his life. The goal never waivers, but a wide focus is always in play, and this allows the team to dodge obstacles and take advantage of breaks that come its way.

A wide focus presents a big, clear picture, which lets you be aware of *all* variables. This is a terrific advantage. It helps you distinguish and attract advantageous prospects while being aware of potential disasters. That's why a wide focus is your best strategy.

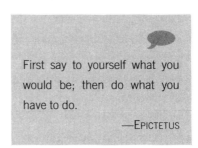

First say to yourself what you would be; then do what you have to do.

—EPICTETUS

Planning versus Strategizing

Guess what? They're not the same thing.

Planning is about projecting and laying out an agenda for what you want to have happen. The plan Rob and I shared was to bike to the bottom of the hill.

Strategy is having a clear vision of how you will actually operate; that is, keeping a wide focus in case things change (believe me, they will) and being ready for them while never losing sight of your goal. On my bike ride, I didn't use a strategy. I didn't keep an eye out for changes along the way, so I wasn't prepared for them. That's why I tumbled.

Strategy permits you to be aware of events you may have never even thought of when you set your original plan. It's about giving up a rigid mind-set and allowing yourself to be innovative at all times. In other words, acknowledging that one plan doesn't fit all situations. It's like when people hear a certain kind of scenario and say, "This is how I'd react." No one really knows how they're going to react until faced with the situation. That's why it's best to let your mind (and your plan) expand to work with the challenges and opportunities along the way. It's kind of a mental go-with-the-flow.

With strategy you can maneuver around the bumps and swing into a detour if one comes up. That's how strategy helps you achieve a faster outcome with less effort.

Think about how a general operates. Yes, he has an objective, but he doesn't order, "This is how we are going to proceed no matter what." He realizes that in the event that the enemy makes a surprise attack, he can and will shift his tactics. That is part of his strategy. At the same time, his intention—to win—never waivers.

Since you are the general of your goals, first you must clarify your final outcome. (And, as we discussed in the previous chapter, you will then also have a much better chance of seeing circumstances that may help you create luck.)

Next, you must always be aware of both your obstacles and your opportunities. With a clear final result firmly in mind, you will be able to make better choices.

Finally, always remember that to support your strategy, you must constantly observe and interpret results to see if change is necessary.

Seven Strategic Steps for Extreme Success

1. Think about what success really means for you. Determine what you truly want for an outcome in your business or your life.

2. See, feel, experience, and be able to articulate your vision as if it's already happened.

3. Look at what benefits your vision holds for you and for others.

4. Create your strategy with the mind-set of, How might I achieve this with greater ease?

5. Look for the highest possible return on the lowest investment of time, resources, and effort.

6. Be as aware and as curious as possible.

7. Be bold and act on opportunities.

When you overplan and focus on the small stuff, you shrink your world and end up struggling.

When you're clear on your outcome and employ a wide-focus strategy to reach it, you can better anticipate obstacles, take advantage of opportunities, and succeed with greater ease.

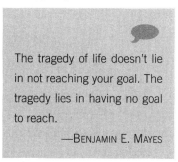

The tragedy of life doesn't lie in not reaching your goal. The tragedy lies in having no goal to reach.

—BENJAMIN E. MAYES

Row, Row, Row Your Boat

Imagine you're floating down a river on a raft. As you bob along toward your intention (let's say a lake), you gently maneuver around barriers such as rocks and trees. At the same time, you make the most of what comes your way, like locating the current and flowing with it. You don't have to figure out all your turns ahead of time because you know the general direction to the lake. You simply flow with the intention of getting there as you constantly scan the way ahead to check for potential difficulties and possibilities.

That's what my client Maria learned to do. She hired me as her coach because she wanted to grow her e-commerce consulting business. During our first session we discovered that she was stuck in the limited view of overplanning tasks and to-do's. She put so much focus on preparation and getting ready that she wasn't putting any energy into finding ways to expand her success. Not only that: The effort of micro-focusing was exhausting her.

After a few coaching sessions, where we looked deeper at how she was operating, she shifted out of her micro-planning mind-set and the "big picture" came back into focus.

Suddenly she said, "I'm not making money by planning. It's not about paper . . . it's about connecting with people."

When I asked, "How could you do that with greater ease?" she began to tell me about prospects that were right under her nose. She mentioned her current resources and realized that those readily available connections might be able to help her.

Then I asked, "What do you have now that could help you create more income?"

"My income is going to come from those people," she stated as she clearly saw her existing resources sitting right in the middle of the big picture. She achieved some fantastic results. Contacting several friends and business acquaintances, she told them she wanted to expand her business. She explained what type of client she was looking for and how she wanted to work.

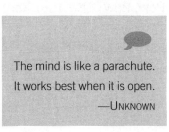

The mind is like a parachute. It works best when it is open.
—UNKNOWN

Within one month, Maria had teamed up with a hot new

consulting firm, and landed a large contract with the VISA Corporation.

Reality Check

What do you usually do to avoid taking action on what you see as a scary or challenging step toward your goals?

How do you remind yourself of your intentions when the going gets tough?

What is one action you could take right now that doesn't have to do with paper or planning?

Keepers: Thoughts to Remember

➤ Planning is about projecting and laying out an agenda for what you want to happen. Strategy is having a clear vision of how you will actually operate; that is, keeping a wide focus in case things change while never losing sight of your goal.

➤ Strategy permits you to be aware of events you may have never even thought of when you set your original plan. It allows you to be flexible and innovative.

➤ When you overplan and focus on the small stuff, you shrink your world and you will struggle.

➤ If you put too much energy on preparation, you won't have the energy to take action.

➤ To support your strategy, you must constantly observe and interpret results to see if change is necessary.

➤ Use the Seven Strategic Steps for Extreme Success.

Action Idea #20: Experience Wide Focus

To practice the skill of wide focus, take a five-minute walk and be aware and curious. Often we mentally check out. We end up thinking about the past or the future at the expense of seeing what is around us now. As you walk, practice being fully present.

Begin your walk with an intention to notice certain things: such as each tree you pass, each intersection you cross, or each person you make eye contact with. This is the same type of mindfulness that will help you notice opportunities that can move you toward your goals. Your ability to maintain a wide focus will improve with practice.

PART 5

Make FEAR Your Friend

12

Intention Attention

I am always doing things I can't do; that's how I get to do them.

—Pablo Picasso

It's time to take the ultimate challenge.

Wait just a minute, Rich, you might be thinking. I know how important it is to stop struggling. I learned how to create intentional luck. I can prepare myself for greater effectiveness, and I've seen my vision, so I'm really aware of what I want to work toward. Now what do you want me to do? Climb a mountain or ski off a cliff or skydive, too?

Actually, no. *The most extreme sport we all face (and which I think of as an equal-opportunity obstacle) is confronting our fear.*

Here is what I want you to do right now: Refer back to your Life Balance Wheel and see where you still aren't satisfied. Something is holding you back from achieving fulfillment in those areas. Most likely that "thing" is fear.

Back in chapter 4 I asked you:

➥ What is a current change you could make in your life that you've been avoiding because it is scary or uncomfortable?

➤ What are you afraid of?

➤ What would you do if you had no fear?

➤ How might this change affect your success?

Now that you've gained more clarity on your future vision, are the answers still the same? Back then I didn't ask you to take any action, but that was then and this is now. It's time to meet your fear head-on and take a step—no matter how small—toward your dreams and goals.

Fear is a frequent companion on the path of personal change. In my work as a coach, a workshop facilitator, and as someone who regularly dares himself to leave his comfort zone, I've seen all types of fears and heard every type of excuse for not achieving an intention.

If you *really* want to succeed, you must face those fears and challenges that are currently holding you back. Avoiding your fears is a losing strategy. When you allow your fears to keep you from achieving what you really want, it can do a number on your self-esteem. Backing away only makes your fear worse. You might get short-term relief now, but you will struggle later when that fear rises up again—and it will.

And fear is sneaky! It disguises itself in many forms: resistance, avoidance, procrastination—the list goes on. That's why fears *must* be addressed. Even if ignored, they will still be there in the background controlling many decisions and preventing you from fully participating in your life. If you don't recognize fear, or if you deny it, then fear will control you.

It comes down to this: You must risk getting out of your comfort zone in order to achieve Extreme Success. That means thinking and doing things differently to get better results.

Believe me, I do understand resistance and fear because, when it's time for action, that's when dread shows up. As you've probably noticed, my extreme sports stories always include one feeling—fear!

I feel fear before I bungee jump, climb, or skydive. I also experience fear when I am about to give a keynote speech, do a national media interview, or introduce myself at some big business networking event. Why do I have that fear? It doesn't matter. What does matter is that I acknowledge my fear. I look at what it's saying to me. Then I find a way to progress through it toward the outcome I desire.

So whether I challenge myself with a physical risk (accompanied by a high measure of built-in safety backups) or one that involves business or my personal life, the real test is dealing with the mental fear that accompanies it.

That's why this part of the book is going to show you new and different ways to address what is holding you back. Even if you know exactly what you want, that powerful four-letter emotion can act as a restraint.

Despite all that, you *can* turn fear into an energizing force. You can train your brain to process fear a new way. Learning to calm your mind when you are staring fear in the face is a powerful strategy and a terrific advantage, because the better you are at working *with* your fear, the faster and easier you will move toward Extreme Success.

To do that, I've developed a four-step process. In the world of Extreme Success here's what fear means.

F—Focus your attention on your intention.
E—Explore your fear.
A—Assess your options and your assets.
R—Respond with yes or no.

In previous chapters I talked about the importance of focus. When dealing with fear, the power of focus continues. Here's why: When you concentrate your energy and attention on what you want (instead of getting stuck thinking about the worst thing that can happen), you have a *reason* to take the necessary risks to get what you want.

So in this chapter I'll go over *focus.* Chapter 13 will cover *explore,* chapter 14 will discuss *assess,* and chapter 15 will delve into *respond.* To show how the process works, I'm going to use one of my extreme sports stories, along with the progress of one of my clients, through all of these chapters. That way you'll see how each part of the method works.

It's time to take action and overcome your fear. It's all that stands between you and Extreme Success.

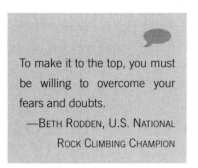

To make it to the top, you must be willing to overcome your fears and doubts.
—BETH RODDEN, U.S. NATIONAL ROCK CLIMBING CHAMPION

Focus Begins on the Inside

Seven hundred and thirty feet is a long way down.

That's what ran through my head as our crew drove toward Foresthill Bridge in Auburn, California, the third-highest bridge in America. This was *Extreme Weekend.* Six guys, one girl, and an intention to bungee jump off three of the nation's most spectacular bridges in two days. The next day we would head out to a stunning train trestle and then drive to the Golden Gate Bridge.

It was one o'clock in the morning as we walked carefully along the steel mesh catwalk of Foresthill Bridge. A full moon gave us pretty good visibility. When I glanced down I could see the deep canyon far below with what looked like a little stream running through it. Later I found out that the little stream was over fifty feet wide.

Several days before, my brother Steve had explained that I'd be accelerating 9.8 meters per second squared, which is faster than *any* sports car on the road today—about 0 to 90 miles per hour in four seconds. The highest jump I had ever done was 250 feet, so my insides were squirting adrenaline like a water pistol. Butterflies took flight in my stomach and all I could think was, Rich, when you jump, do not yell "Mommy!"

As I lowered hundreds of feet of bungee cord off the side of the bridge, two guys secured the other end to several of the crossbeams. Everything was tripled up. Even if lightning struck any part of our system, we still had two more backups to keep us from taking the last dip of our lives in the river below.

Then I heard Greg. "Okay, Rich, you're on!"

As I strapped the two orange harnesses around my ankles, a spooky visual flashed through my mind. I saw a tombstone that read RICH FETTKE: FEBRUARY 23, 1964–JULY 9, 1994. I quickly shifted my attention back to the buckles on my harnesses. My heart started beating faster, and within moments my mouth felt like it was stuffed with cotton balls.

Steve duct-taped a two-way radio to my upper arm so I could communicate with our crew once I had completed my jump and the rebounds slowed down.

I must have looked like a zombie as I climbed over the handrail of the catwalk and edged out along the foot-wide girder that took me to the outer edge of the bridge. I felt a buzz pass through my body like a low-level electrical current.

"Ready for a countdown?" Greg asked. That cued me to

remember my process of overcoming fear. I did what Steve had told me many times on other jumps: "Don't focus on the fall before you jump or else you'll concentrate on your fear. Pick a tree across the canyon, Make that your goal. Focus on that tree and jump toward it with all you've got."

I chose a tree and my confidence began to rise.

This was step one for me to deal with my fear. I used *focus.*

I looked at the outcome I aimed to achieve and it reminded me why I was about to take this leap. I wanted to push my limits, expand my perspectives, and build my courage muscle even more. I wanted the rush and the

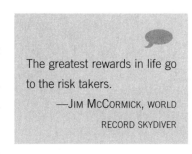

The greatest rewards in life go to the risk takers.

—JIM McCORMICK, WORLD RECORD SKYDIVER

exhilaration that comes from pushing my mind to the limit. (You'll see how I explored my fear in chapter 13.)

Focus Trumps Fear Every Time

Steve's advice worked wonders. It allowed me to focus my energy on what I wanted instead of on what I feared. (It gave me something positive to concentrate on.) When I did that, my fear backed off and I was able to think more clearly and be more present in the moment.

The fear pathway doesn't change much from situation to situation. In my jump, I:

➤ knew I was going to take a risk and do something I had never done before, so my body responded with an adrenaline rush;

➤ was afraid I was going to die or at least get hurt;

➤ identified an object and "aimed" for it as my goal, in other words *I focused my attention on my intention.* By having something positive to focus on that represented my goal, I immediately found direction.

Your Built-in Fear-Handling Fuel

When you are afraid, your body responds with its own form of rocket fuel: adrenaline.

Adrenaline is one of the natural hormones your body releases when you push limits or you are confronted with a challenge. Adrenaline flows through your body, giving you extra awareness, mental clarity, and the physical ability to respond quickly to different situations. Colors are sharper, sounds are clearer. You are more conscious of odors, and your body feels energized.

Whether you are jumping out of a plane or setting up a sales presentation with your hottest prospect, if the activity scares you, adrenaline will provide you with the strength you need to succeed. By recognizing how you feel when adrenaline is coursing through your veins, you will become much more skilled at using this ally to your advantage by employing it to accomplish a goal.

At the same time you should be aware that adrenaline also kicks in when you are under any kind of stress—from getting caught in traffic to dealing with difficult people. In these everyday situations, adrenaline can burn you out, because your body doesn't get a chance to rest and recuperate.

I used to get tense from adrenaline in all kinds of circumstances. Now, because I've gotten used to the feeling through extreme sports, I can say, "Ah, I know this feeling. It's adrenaline. I need to be aware of why I'm feeling it. Am I facing a real risk, or do I just need to reduce the number of stressful events that I tolerate in my life? Maybe I need to leave a little earlier to avoid traffic, or perhaps I should discuss what's bothering me with a friend."

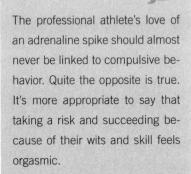

The professional athlete's love of an adrenaline spike should almost never be linked to compulsive behavior. Quite the opposite is true. It's more appropriate to say that taking a risk and succeeding because of their wits and skill feels orgasmic.

—MARYANN KARINCH, *LESSONS FROM THE EDGE*

By learning how adrenaline feels, you can use it instead of it using you.

Paul's Tree Across the Canyon

When he hired me to coach him, Paul, thirty-eight, wanted to move to the next level of his profession. He had started his own financial services company five years earlier and had met his initial goals. For the past two years, however, Paul had hit a plateau.

When I asked what would take him to the next level, he told me that he wanted to move from a commission-based to a fee-based business. He no longer wanted to sell stocks, funds, and insurance and receive a percentage of each sale. Instead, he wanted his clients to pay him an hourly fee to advise them on their investments and to manage their portfolios. This would allow him to choose the best investments for

his clients and at the same time allow him to work with a
more affluent clientele.

I asked Paul how he could achieve this goal. He told me
that one of the best ways was to begin speaking for groups of
his target client profile, which consisted mostly of business
owners and entrepreneurs. Paul's strategy was clear, yet he
had been resisting taking the next step for over a year.

"Are you ready to do something about this now?" I asked.

"Yes—but I don't want to be," he replied. "The truth is that
I'm terrified of public speaking. I used to have no problem
with it in college, but that was ten years ago. Now I think I'd
puke if I got up in front of a room to give a talk."

(This was not a big surprise. I've read several surveys
where people ranked public speaking as their number-one
greatest fear—higher even than death!)

I said, "Instead of creating a nightmare about this, let's
look at a positive fantasy. Tell me about the best possible outcome you can imagine if you began speaking and everything
went well."

Paul's whole tone changed, and his energy perked up
when he said, "Well, if everything went well, I'd be speaking
to local groups of business owners and entrepreneurs who
have lots of money to invest but are not sure of how or
where to invest it. I'd teach them ways that they could grow
their income without the risk that usually holds novice in-
vestors back from making a great return on their money.

"Then several of those people would want to hire me because they would see how incredibly brilliant I am." He
chuckled. "The word would spread and other successful
people would start calling me up and begging me to work
with them. I'd be helping these clients and they would be
helping me. I love it."

Paul had just gone through the first step of overcoming a

fear that had been paralyzing his progress. His "tree across the canyon" was a thriving business full of ideal clients whom he attracted with fun and ease. *He had his focus on the positive outcome he wanted to accomplish.*

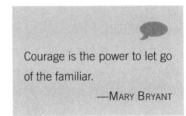

Courage is the power to let go of the familiar.

—Mary Bryant

In the next chapter you'll see what happens when Paul explores his fears.

Keepers: Thoughts to Remember

➤ On the path of personal change, fear is a frequent companion, but not an enemy.

➤ If you want to succeed, you must face the fears and challenges that are currently holding you back.

➤ When you allow your fears to keep you from achieving what you really want, it can do a number on your self-esteem.

➤ Backing away only makes your fear worse. You might get short-term relief now, but you will struggle later when that fear rises up again.

➤ If you don't recognize fear, or you deny it, then fear will control you.

➤ You *can* turn fear into an energizing force. The better you are at working *with* your fear, the faster and easier you will move toward Extreme Success.

➤ Focusing on your intention allows you to target your energy on what you want instead of on what you fear.

➤ If an activity scares you, adrenaline will help provide you with the strength you need to succeed. By learning what adrenaline feels like, you can better use *it* instead of it using *you*.

➤ In the world of Extreme Success here's what FEAR means:

F—Focus your attention on your intention.
E—Explore your fear.
A—Assess your options and your assets.
R—Respond with Yes or No.

Action Idea #21: Understand How Fear Works

To get a better understanding of how you handle fear, answer the following questions.

1. What is the scariest thing you've ever done?
2. Why did you do it?
3. What was your fear telling you?
4. What were you focusing on?
5. What could you have focused on to reduce your fear?
6. What did you learn about yourself and your fears?

13

Dance with Your Protector

He who fears he shall suffer already suffers what he fears.

—Montaigne

In several of the previous chapters you've heard me mention the "voice of fear," a.k.a. the "inner voice" or "the Protector." Well, it's time to get up close and personal with the Protector and *explore* that insistent mental mouthpiece that speaks up whenever you are about to step out of your comfort zone. After coaching hundreds of clients, from CEOs to homemakers, I can say that it seems as though just about everyone has some type of "inner voice" that screams for attention. The fear of change rarely fails to get a rise out of the Protector.

While you might regard the Protector as a nasty beast bent on trying to prevent you from reaching your goals and dreams, in reality it is your ally. Its job is to warn "Danger! Danger!" whenever it feels that you—and it—are in harm's way. Yeah, I know the "old school" way to deal with fear was to ignore it, push through it, or fight it. I want to show you a new way, which is about awareness and mindfulness. It's about using your fear as an asset and regarding it as your partner.

By doing this you'll discover the resistance that holds you back by listening to what the Protector is trying to tell you. You'll get the opportunity to *explore* the real reasons behind the questions "What is stopping me?" or "What fear is coming up concerning this change?"

Fear gives you the chance to check out the situation and look at all kinds of possibilities. Then you can decide rationally if it's a good idea to move ahead. That's why partnering with your Protector is the most practical way of exploring your fear.

Fear: Your Unlikely Partner

You and your Protector are a package deal; it was born with you. Ever since then it has done its best to safeguard you from harm, embarrassment, and ridicule. Every time you failed at something, your Protector was there to remember it and believes its job is to keep similar episodes from happening again. It aids you by acting like an internal stop sign that signals you to halt to protect you from potential massive failure and loss.

The problem is the Protector often *overdoes* it because it doesn't realize that things may be different today than they were in the past.

If you ever heard negative commentary in your head such as "You can't do that," "You're going to fail," or "That will hurt you," then it's time to begin the process of partnering with your Protector. Tell it that you're listening and you want to know what it is trying to protect you from. Let it know your intention and ask it, "How can I have what I want and still honor your concerns?"

When you do this, you will get an answer and your Protector will settle down. Remember: Your Protector is your enemy *only* if you view it that way. **When you partner with your fear, you achieve your goals with greater ease.**

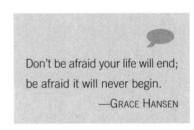

Don't be afraid your life will end; be afraid it will never begin.

—GRACE HANSEN

Yielding Gives You Power

One of my friends once told me about something she saw in Hong Kong. The scaffolding around buildings going up were constructed of bamboo. The reason? It was strong, but it yielded. That meant it would bend with the wind, instead of staying rigid and snapping under the pressure. This quality gave the bamboo much value, because it "knew" when to "give" in order to preserve its strength.

The same principle applies to aikido, where the first step is learning the skill of blending. In doing so, you step to the side and allow your attacker's energy to pass you by. Then you seize that energy and direct it where you want it to go.

It's no different when you explore your fear. By giving way to your fear instead of fighting against it, you tap into your Protector's energy. By allowing your fear to prompt you toward finding the smartest, safest, and most effective way toward your intention, you can achieve your goal without struggle.

Ask Your Fear to Dance

When I speak to an audience I often do the following exercise, which I call the Protector Dance. I ask a volunteer to come up on the stage and, after finding out his or her name, ask the person to represent my fear. Let's call my helper Chris.

I tell the audience, "Let's imagine that Chris is the voice inside my head that tells me I'm going to be harmed or I'm going to fail. Now, over there is my goal," I say as I point to a table or a chair. "What I want you to do, Chris, is to try to hold me back from my goal, actually get in my way and keep me from reaching it."

As I start to walk toward my goal, Chris blocks my way or takes hold of my arms and pushes me back. As I push back against Chris, I say, "Okay, freeze. Look what's happening here. Where am I putting my attention?"

The crowd replies, "On your fear."

"Yes!" I exclaim. "And where is my energy going?"

"On your fear!" the crowd roars.

"Exactly! And now I'm going to show you how to partner *with* fear.

"Okay, Chris," I say. "Let's try that again." As I walk toward my goal and my fear gets in my way I state, "Fear, I notice you have something to say about this. What is it?"

At this point the volunteer usually says something like, "You are not prepared," or "You're going to be embarrassed," or "You don't have enough time."

My answer, directed at Chris is, "Thanks for letting me know. Let's look at what needs to be done so that none of those things happen." Then I maneuver us into a waltz position and we begin to dance in clockwise rotations over toward my goal. (As you can imagine, if the volunteer is a man the audience is usually laughing pretty hard at this point.)

Chris and I dance over to my goal and I touch it. At this point the audience *always* applauds. Then I say, "Please give Chris, my fear, a hand."

After the applause dies down I say, "Do you see the difference between fighting our fears and dancing with them? When we partner with our fear, we can understand what it needs for us to move forward. When we resist or fight our fears, we end up struggling and using lots of energy that doesn't get us where we want to go."

It's Time to Explore My Fear

When you last saw me on Foresthill Bridge I was focusing on my goal. I chose a tree to represent my intention, and my confidence began to rise.

I did another check on my harnesses because I needed to make sure I was properly hooked to the cord. I also needed to examine some other things—like making sure that the other end of the cord was hooked to the bridge! Everything looked good and I felt even more confidence build. Then I went over what I planned to do when the countdown started.

This is the time when I explored my fear by addressing it. My first thought was, Okay, fear, what do you need from me? What are you asking for?

The answer I received was, "I'm getting a reading in the red zone here! What is the chance of injury? Did you check all your equipment properly? Are we going to die?"

"No," I told my Protector firmly. "We're not. I know what to focus on—the tree, the symbol of pushing my limits. I've checked and rechecked my safeguards. I'm ready to assess my options before I jump."

See, I knew my Protector would make itself heard—and that was fine with me. It had already made itself known by giving me an advance showing of my "tombstone." Checking in with my fear helped me avoid being freaked out and

not going after what I wanted. All the Protector wanted was
to be recognized and spoken to logically and honestly. (In
chapter 14 you'll see how I assessed my options now that my
Protector and I were working as a team.)

At this point on the bridge I:

➤ acknowledged my fear;

➤ *explored my fear* by talking to and listening to my Protector;

➤ shifted my attention to my safety measures and checked them once more.

Paul Explores Talking to His Fear

Remember Paul from the last chapter? After he had described
his positive fantasy about building his financial services business, I knew there was more for us to look at. Yes, he held
new excitement about the possibilities of speaking for his target market, but when I asked him, "So what's your fear saying about this?" Paul froze. He went into silent mode again
and tried to change the subject.

"Actually, I don't think I'm ready to go out and speak yet. I
still have a bunch of stuff I need to learn if I'm going to start
giving seminars about investing."

"Like what?" I asked.

"Well . . . like . . . um . . . you know . . . stuff."

"Sounds like your fear's got something to say about this,
doesn't it?"

"Yes," Paul admitted. "I guess it does."

It was time for Paul to make friends with his fear instead of trying to run away from it or fight it. So I said, "I'd like to have a conversation with your fear. Are you willing to do that with me?"

"Okay," Paul replied. "How are we going to do that?"

"Just close your eyes and trust me," I instructed. "Take a few deep breaths. I want both of us to communicate with this fear that's telling you not to speak in front of a group. Right now, imagine that you're having a conversation with your fear. Let it know that in no way are you trying to ignore it or destroy it.

"Ask your fear to present itself by giving you a feeling somewhere in your body." I paused.

Paul said, "I feel it in my stomach."

"Good. Now thank your fear for communicating with us."

"Thanks for showing up, Mr. Fear," Paul said.

"Tell your fear—again—that you want to listen to it and you have no intention of ignoring or destroying it." I paused as Paul did so. "Inform your fear that there is something you need to know. You want to find out what your fear requires to be able to allow you to achieve your goal. Now ask your fear why it doesn't want you to speak in front of a group."

There was a long silence. Finally Paul answered. "It said, 'Because the last time you did you screwed up.' "

"Okay, tell me more," I prompted.

"In my senior year of college I gave a talk in my business policy class without being prepared and I got totally lost. I felt like an idiot. I also got a lousy grade."

"No wonder your fear is coming up again," I said. "Do you think the same thing might happen now if you talked to a group?"

"I wouldn't be surprised."

"And if you spoke without being prepared and got lost, what do you imagine might happen then?"

"Well, probably the same thing as in college. I'd feel like an idiot and I wouldn't get the new clients I was hoping for."

"And then what do you imagine might happen?"

"Then I might even lose some of the clients I have now, because their friends would say what an idiot I am."

"And then what?"

"Well, then I'd go broke and I'd be on the street begging people for money and shivering through the night with no place to live." Paul let out a big laugh and said, "That's pretty doomsday sounding, isn't it?"

"Hey, if that's what your fear is telling you, no wonder you've been avoiding public speaking. Let's look at what options you do have as you move forward."

By exploring his fears, Paul found out what was holding him back. His Protector wanted to make sure he was aware of possible challenges and obstacles on the way to achieving his goal.

Keepers: Thoughts to Remember

➤ The "old school" way to deal with fear was to ignore it or fight it. The new way is about using your fear as an asset.

➤ Fear gives you the chance to check out the situation and look at all kinds of possibilities.

➤ Your Protector helps you by acting like an internal stop sign that identifies potential failure. The problem is the Protector often *overdoes* it.

➤ Your Protector is your enemy only if you view it that way.

➤ By allowing your fear to prompt you toward finding the smartest, safest, and most effective way toward your intention, you can achieve your goal without struggle.

➤ When you partner with your fear, you can understand what it needs for you to move forward.

➤ When you *explore* your fear you:

—acknowledge the particular terrors that have arisen;

—hear what the Protector has to say;

—learn what the Protector needs from you.

Action Idea #22: Explore Your Fear

Take five minutes to sit in silence. Then ask your Protector to tell you what it needs in order for you to accomplish your goals. Don't try to manipulate or battle your Protector—it will probably win. Instead, tell it what you want to achieve and ask how you can move toward that while still honoring your Protector's concerns.

Here are the steps for partnering with your fear. Read it through a few times before you do it.

1. Close your eyes and ask your fear to communicate with you. Let it know that in no way are you trying to ignore or destroy it.

2. Ask your fear to present itself by giving you a feeling somewhere in your body. Pay attention and you will notice it.

3. Once you get that feeling, thank your fear for communicating with you.

4. Tell your fear what your goal is and let it know that you want to hear, and be aware of, its concerns before you move forward.

5. Thank your fear for communicating with you and reassure it that you will continue to listen to its concerns instead of trying to fight, ignore, or destroy it.

6. Ask your fear what it needs for you to progress toward your goal. What options do you have? Tell your fear you are going to assess those options to choose the one that seems to work best.

14

Assess the Situation

The first act of self-responsibility, and the base of all the others, is the act of taking responsibility for being conscious—that is, of bringing an appropriate awareness to our activities.

—Nathaniel Branden, author of *Taking Responsibility*

Fear is taking on a whole new meaning, isn't it? Now that you know how to focus and explore, it's time to learn how to assess. This is the step where you evaluate what you discovered when you listened to your Protector.

When you assess a situation, you check the chance of any massive failure, loss, or pain. From there you can discover the different options available for moving forward with your goals.

Coming up with specific actions is the key to this step. Many folks get clear on their vision, and then fear stops them in their tracks. Basically, they have an "Aha" experience but don't do anything with their discoveries. This is where the skill of breaking down big goals into smaller, achievable actions is so helpful. At the same time it takes the concerns of your Protector into consideration. This is also a good time to assess the different ways you can get support and accountability.

When you assess, you first ask yourself, "What *can* I do?

What are my options here? Which seem to be the best steps for me to take?"

From there you can create action steps based on your self-research. The answers you come up with will be carried forward into *respond*, the next and final step of the F.E.A.R. process.

When you take the time to assess your options, you manage your fear instead of letting your fear control you.

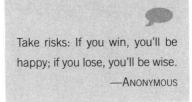

Take risks: If you win, you'll be happy; if you lose, you'll be wise.
—ANONYMOUS

I Assess What to Do Next

When you last saw me on Foresthill Bridge, I went over what I planned to do when the countdown started.

This is the time when I assessed my options and clarified what I wanted to do. I did have choices: I could have tied on a blindfold or jumped off the bridge backward—or both. Or I could have asked two of my fellow jumpers to give me a push at some point during the countdown.

So far I had:

➤ *focused* on a goal that represented my intention, which was to make this jump and gain the thrill and courage that would come from it.

➤ *explored* my fear, listened to my Protector's concerns, and come to terms with it. My fear told me not to get injured or killed. Then it informed me that it was okay to move forward as long as I double-checked my safety measures and knew what I had to do before, during, and after my jump. I had clarified ahead of time how I wanted to operate when fear showed up. In this way I partnered with my fear instead of fighting against it.

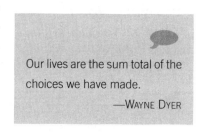 assessed my options by looking at the different ways I could jump. After I had reviewed my choices I came up with a basic strategy. I:

—decided that I wanted to jump forward without a blindfold;

—came up with several steps associated with the countdown.

When the jumper gives the word, everyone on the bridge joins in and counts down from five. On "one" the jumper (usually) takes the leap. My strategy was when I heard "five" I would focus on the tree across the canyon, on "four" I'd take a deep breath, on "three" I'd refocus on the tree, on "two" I'd bend my knees and pull my arms back, and on "one" I'd leap toward the tree with everything I had.

Now it was time for me to respond to my plan, to say either yes or no to it.

> Our lives are the sum total of the choices we have made.
>
> —WAYNE DYER

Paul Assesses His Options

After Paul and I explored his fear and realized why he was afraid of public speaking, I made the following request:

"Paul, thank your fear again for letting you know what to look out for." Paul did so.

Then I said, "Let your fear know that growing your business is important to you and ask it how you can move forward while at the same time honoring its concerns."

Paul was quiet for a moment. Then he said, "My fear is telling me that it will allow me to proceed if I promise to be prepared for my next talk."

"Great. Now ask it what 'prepared' means. How prepped do you have to be?"

Paul paused and then replied, "If I give the talk to my wife and a friend, and they say it is ready for the public, then that will be enough proof that I am ready."

"What else do we need to look at as far as your speaking goes?"

"I need to book a date, find a place to give the talk, and begin to prepare what I'm going to say."

I worked with Paul so that he had a clear strategy for achieving his goal. When it was done I asked him, "How committed are you to this plan?"

"One hundred percent," he answered.

Paul and I had gone through the first three steps of turning his fear into success. So far he had:

➤ *focused* on the positive outcome he wanted to accomplish; that is, to build his business through speaking.

➤ *explored* his fear to find out what was holding him back and to make sure he was aware of possible challenges and obstacles. His fear told him not to look like an idiot, fail, or throw up. Then his fear told him that it is okay to move ahead as long as he promised to be prepared.

➤ *assessed* the different options that could help him take the steps toward his goals. Figuring out how he could prepare himself, Paul looked at what options he had including who to invite and if he wanted to charge for his seminar or give it for free. He also considered the option of doing his presentation with another person, such as an estate planner or an accountant. After Paul assessed these possibilities he came up with his action plan. He:

—identified the date on which to hold the seminar;

—came up with three different potential locations for the event;

—decided that he wanted to do this first appearance on his own;

—chose to offer his seminar for no fee.

In the next chapter we'll look at how Paul responded to his choices.

Keepers: Thoughts to Remember

➤ When you assess a situation, you check the chance of any massive failure, loss, or pain. From there you can discover the different options available for moving forward with your goals.

➤ When you assess, you first ask yourself, "What *can* I do? What are my options here? Which seem to be the best steps for me to take?" From there you can create an action plan based on your self-research.

➤ When you take the time to assess your options, you control your fear instead of letting your fear control you.

Action Idea #23: Take Stock

Now that you've looked at what you want and explored your fears, let's look at what options you have as you move forward. Write down any possible steps that could help you achieve your intention. Don't forget to partner with your Protector for its input. Your Protector may offer some ideas that you haven't thought of. Make sure you do this. If you don't, there's a good chance you'll have to deal with your Protector later . . . and then it might not be so helpful.

After you come up with possible options, assess which seem to be the best steps. In the next chapter we'll look at taking the leap and staying committed.

15

→

Take the Plunge

You can either take action or you can hang back and hope for a miracle.
—Peter F. Drucker

Congratulations! You know how to focus, explore, and assess your fear. Now it's time to respond to it. You must ask yourself, "What *will* I do?"

The reason I'm asking you to pose this question is this: Actions follow thoughts. When you ask yourself, "What will I do?" you draw out a choice of either "go ahead" or "don't do it."

If you want to be successful in any goal, you must jump with all you've got. That's why you must make a choice. A halfhearted leap won't get you where you want to go—and you might hurt yourself in the process.

The response will tell you if you're ready to say yes or no to taking action. If you're not, don't force it. Go back through chapters 12, 13, and 14 and revisit each step. You might discover that your Protector feels like it was not part of this choice. If so, it may not embrace the changes you must make. So retrace the steps and discover what needs to happen for you to succeed.

On the other hand, if the answer is yes, then go for it—and expect the best.

The important thing to remember is this: No matter how long it takes, in order to achieve Extreme Success you must eventually respond yes to your choice.

The P Word

International speaker Rosita Perez has a great rhyme that goes, "One for the money, two for the show, three to get ready, three to get ready, three to get ready . . ."

Can you relate? Many people get stuck when they start to think, Should I do it? Maybe I should. Maybe I shouldn't. The gray area between yes and no, which clouds your mind with indecision and frustration, is easy to get stuck in. This twilight zone is known as procrastination, an approach that can stifle your progress toward your dreams and goals. When you are stuck in the procrastination pit, your energy can get zapped out of you faster than electricity from a California power plant.

The best way to overcome procrastination is to make a simple choice, either yes or no. Proactive as opposed to reactive, choice implies responsibility. You're either going to discover what is holding you back and act on it or move ahead right now. It's as straightforward as that.

Commit Your Mind, and Your Body Will Follow

One of the most powerful ways to "lock in" a commitment is to connect your mental commitment to a physical action. I do this when I take a group through an activity-based workshop. I've used ropes courses, bungee jumping, skydiving, and rock climbing to help clients secure their commitments.

During a rock climb, for instance, I challenge each participant to put on a harness and climb a rock wall, either outdoors or inside at a rock climbing gym. This experience helps people realize the incredible potential they have within. Each person gets a chance to experience what it feels like to overcome fear and to perform a physical activity that is a powerful metaphor for going after his or her goals and dreams.

Before a rock climb I ask each participant to write down his or her main intention for the following ninety days. Then I climb up and put the first participant's piece of paper at the top. After I come back down, I say, "This climb represents the journey toward your goal. At the top is your intention. You can make it a struggle or you can make it a fun challenge. It's up to you. Ask your team for support and encouragement. Ask them to point out holds that you might not see. Once you get to the top, grab your goal, and do whatever you want to celebrate. You can yell, pray, scream. However you want to celebrate is up to you."

Then I give the first climber the next person's goal and the process is repeated. It is amazing what happens. People laugh, cry, tremble, and hug each other. Afterward, when we debrief this event, there are always fantastic comparisons from the group. They talk about how the climb is so much like the way they live their lives.

You can participate in a similar experience. Although it's not as adrenaline producing as an extreme sport, it can still have a memorable impact on your personal commitment to your goals and help you move from resistance and fear to action and achievement.

When you have gone through *focus, explore,* and *assess* and you're ready to respond with a yes to your intention, write down your goal and what you want to say yes to. Then, locate a line on the floor, either where the rug meets the floor or some other visible line that divides two spaces. One side of the line represents where you are and what you have. The other side represents where you want to be and what you want.

If you're ready to make a 100 percent commitment to your intention, step over the line. Now please, make this real. I've done this exercise with many groups. Some participants treat it like just another game, whereas some folks really make the most of it. I'm asking you to take it seriously and make it work for you. When you really take the time to look at your commitment, state it out loud, and then step over the line, you can shift from *wanting* to achieve your intention to *knowing* you will achieve it.

You can do it alone in the privacy of your living room, with your Success Partner, or, even better, with a group of people. Each person takes a turn stepping to (and then over) the line and the rest of the group celebrates. There is a lot of power in public declaration.

On the other side of the line I bet you'll experience a surge of courage and commitment. Do it at least once and make your commitment real. Lock it in your body and you'll remember it in your mind.

Safety First, Fun Second

Taking a risk means exposing oneself to potential loss. Some people have told me that they think I harbor a death wish for taking the risks associated with extreme sports. However, the truth is that I have a life wish. I don't want any made-up fears holding me back from going after what I truly value. If I allow resistance and fear to get in the way of my dreams and goals, then I would be selling out on myself. That's why I'm always clear on the risks I want to take.

The fact is, the thrill sports I do are pretty darn safe. Check out these stats. Notice the comparable risks of what is thought of as crazy next to what most people do on a regular basis.

ACTIVITY	RISK OF DEATH/PERSON/YEAR*
Skydiving	1 in 100,000
Bungee jumping	1 in 400,000
Rock climbing	1 in 7,150
Driving an automobile	1 in 5,900
Struck by an automobile	1 in 20,000
Pregnancy	1 in 3,400 (lifetime risk, United States)

Overall, skydiving, bungee jumping, and rock climbing are less likely to kill you than driving a car or expecting a baby! It should also be noted that mistakes in judgment and procedure are the cause of 92 percent of skydiving fatalities.

Furthermore, check out these stats: 72 golfers died in 2.7 million games of golf in 1997 whereas only 36 skydivers died in 2.9 million skydives that year. Almost forty times as many recreational boaters died than amateur skydivers did in 1996. Every year nearly 46,000 people perish in traffic accidents;

*Sources: On skydiving: Data from the *Neue Zuercher Zeitung*, "A Table of Mortality Rates of Different Activities Evaluated with Swiss Statistical Data." On bungee jumping: L. Vaneford and M. Meyers, "Injuries and Bungee Jumping," *Sports Medicine* 20 (1995): 369–74, and P. M. Hite, K. A. Greene, D. I. Levy, et al., "Injuries Resulting from Bungee Cord Jumping," *Annals of Emergency Medicine* 22 (1993): 137–40. Other statistics: B. D. Dinman, "The Reality and Acceptance of Risk," *JAMA* 244 (1980): 1226, and University of Oregon Physics department (1999): http://zebu.uoregon.edu.

approximately 140 die while scuba diving, about 850 lose their lives bicycling, and roughly 80 are killed by lightning. See—fear (or the devil's advocate in your life) often makes up negative fantasies that can hold you back from going after what you really want. So your fears may be based on false assumptions. That's why it's important to explore those notions. You might be creating the invisible wall that keeps you from your intention.

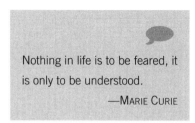

Nothing in life is to be feared, it is only to be understood.

—MARIE CURIE

The Courage to Be Successful

Extreme achievers seek new ways of learning and growing because they do not want to be like everyone else. They hold different beliefs, attitudes, and values. Aiming to grab the most out of life, they know how to work with their fear. Keeping open minds, they are willing to attempt things that others believe are impossible. This is how they excel. They move beyond the average because they understand what it takes to achieve and sustain higher levels of effectiveness and success. Extreme achievers continually test their limits, redefining what they are and pushing themselves to attain seemingly impossible goals.

When you work with your fear and develop your courage you learn to push yourself beyond your normal limits. This is the process of creating a new comfort zone. To prepare yourself for intentional luck and greater courage, you must push your limits and expand your comfort zone on a regular basis.

For example, you don't get to be a great skier by always doing intermediate runs. When you push yourself to do an advanced run, your skill and your confidence improve dramatically.

When your response is yes it's the difference between hoping and having. Many people don't take that leap. I don't think you want to be one of them. I'm figuring that you desire to get the most out of life and you're not going to let anything hold you back from total fulfillment and joy.

Now, when you feel fear, you know it means, "Get ready because you're about to grow—and move to the next level."

I Respond to My Decision

Finally, it was time for me to respond, to say either yes or no. I was either going to jump—or not.

I was ready. I decided that as the countdown went along I'd say, "Yes! Yes! Yes!" over and over to keep a strong focus on my choice.

"Okay, airtime countdown!" I shouted.

Everyone joined in, "Five . . . Four . . . Three . . . Two . . . One . . . Bungeeeeeeeee!" Leaping forward with all of my might I shot out from the bridge and for a moment everything was silent. Then I fell straight down.

Once I jumped, something incredible happened: My fear disappeared! I felt the wind pushing my hair up like Larry's in the Three Stooges. The air sounded like a jet engine as it rushed past my ears. I was falling fast! I felt my stomach in my throat as I let out a big "Yahoooooooooo!"

Suddenly I felt a tug on my ankles. The bungee reached full extension and—*boing!*—I soared back up with the mixed visual of ground, bridge, sky, and stars jiggling through my brain.

After slowly bouncing up and down four or five times, I hung there, dangling like a caught but exhilarated fish. The crew on the bridge dropped a long rope down and I clipped it into my waist harness. Then the motorized winch pulled me back up to the launching point. I climbed back over the rail and onto the catwalk. I felt totally alive, like I could take on *anything*.

After the other jumpers took the leap, we packed up the gear and made our way back toward the parking lot. I remember looking at my watch, and although it read 4:20 A.M. I didn't feel the least bit tired. As we walked, Greg smiled and asked me, "So, are you psyched for the Golden Gate?"

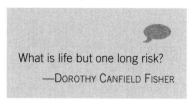

What is life but one long risk?
—DOROTHY CANFIELD FISHER

Paul Responds to His Choice

Now that Paul had *focused, explored,* and *assessed,* it was time for him to *respond* with either a yes or a no. Was he ready to take the leap toward speaking in front of a live audience?

Paul said, "Yes. I'm ready and willing to go for it. We'll have to see how able I am."

To help lock in his commitment, I bet you know what I asked Paul to do. I pointed to where the edge of the rug met the floor. "That is your commitment line," I told him. "The rug side, where you are standing, represents your past. The other side of the line, the floor, symbolizes where you are committed to going, that is, speaking in front of a live audience. In a moment I'm going to ask you to jump over that line to signify physically your one hundred percent commitment to achieving your goal. I'll count from five to one, on one, if you are ready, leap over the line. If you are not ready, don't. If that's your decision, we can investigate your fears some more. Any questions?"

"No. I'm ready."

"Okay," I began, "Five . . . Four . . . Three . . . Two . . . One!" At one, Paul leaped into the air and landed on the floor as he let out a big "Yes!" At that moment I *knew* that Paul was going to achieve his goal.

A short time later, Paul did just that. Having given his speech to his wife and friend and receiving four thumbs up, he booked a conference room at a local hotel. Next he mailed classy invitations to his A-list clients that included an extra invitation to give away. He also invited local business owners whom he had met through the chamber of commerce.

Paul pulled it off! He gave an informative and inspiring seminar on how to make the most of the current economy. After his talk several attendees asked about his services and Paul ended up with three new fee-based clients.

Not surprisingly, Paul was excited when he came to our next coaching session. He said, "I'm definitely proud of myself. I pulled it off and I didn't even puke!" I was proud of Paul, too. Not only had he delivered a great seminar and attracted new clients, he did what he thought he couldn't do. He worked with

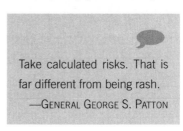

Take calculated risks. That is far different from being rash.
—GENERAL GEORGE S. PATTON

his fear rather than against it, which was one giant step toward extreme success.

➤ Actions follow thoughts.

➤ No matter how long it takes, in order to achieve Extreme Success you must commit 100 percent to moving forward.

➤ The gray area between "yes I will" and "no I won't" is best known as procrastination. Easy to get stuck in, it will zap the energy out of you.

➤ The best way to overcome procrastination is to make a simple choice: yes or no.

➤ One of the most powerful ways to "lock in" a commitment is to connect your mental decision to a physical action.

➤ When you have gone through *focus, explore,* and *assess* and you're ready to say yes to your intention, write down your goal and what you want to say yes to.

➤ To prepare yourself for Extreme Success, you must push your limits and expand your comfort zone on a regular basis.

➤ When you feel fear now, you know it means, "Get ready, because you're about to grow—and move to the next level."

Action Idea #24: Write a Letter to Yourself

Write down a goal that you want to achieve within the next ninety days. Make sure it ties into your main three intentions for the future. Then compose a letter to yourself about why you want to accomplish this goal, what it will feel like once you reach it, how you want to be on the journey toward that goal, and what your fear needs from you as you go for it. Put that letter in a self-addressed stamped envelope, give it to a friend, and ask him or her to mail it to you at some point over the next sixty days.

I've seen how powerful this can be. We often let ourselves "check out" on our commitments and desires. This is one more strategy that you can use to encourage and motivate yourself to have the success you most desire.

Action Idea #25: Expand Your Limits

My challenge is for you to do an activity that pumps your adrenaline level up to at least an 8 on a scale of 10. I know this works! When a person takes a (safe) risk that challenges a fear, he or she can then take that new courage and say, "Hey, if I can _____ [fill in the blank] I can go after this other scary goal that I want to achieve."

Below are several ways that I have seen people confront their fears (and come through with zero injuries but a lot more courage). These activities are actually all very safe. However, many people create negative fantasies about them and therefore build inner fears that hold them back.

➤ go deep-sea fishing or whale watching;

➤ sing karaoke for the first time;

➤ go to the top of a mega-skyscraper and look down;

➤ do a fire walk on hot coals (with a trained professional);

➤ touch a snake at a pet shop (with assistance from an employee);

➤ do a tandem skydive (attached to a professional jumper under the same parachute);

➤ work out at a health club;

➤ do a ropes course seminar;

➤ go for a ride in a private plane or helicopter;

➤ speak at a Toastmasters club, a Speaking Circle, or a similar group;

➤ take the scariest ride at an amusement park;

➤ sign up for and attend a martial arts course;

➤ go on a hot air balloon ride;

➤ take a dance class;

➤ rock climb at an inside climbing gym;

➤ _____ (your ideas?).

Action Idea #26: Revisit FEAR Regularly

Remember to use the FEAR strategy with your Success Partner. It will help you both discover possible resistance to and potholes in the future road to success.

These four simple questions are an excellent tool for either a current challenge or for long-term planning. They will help you break through fear, build courage, and create the results you desire.

F—Focus: "What do you want?"
E—Explore: "What's stopping you?"
A—Assess: "What could you do?"
R—Respond: "What will you do?"

PART 6

Stay in the Zone

16

Momentum Creates Momentum

The ability to concentrate and use your time well is everything.
—Lee Iaccoca, former president of the Chrysler Corporation

Remember Jim, the guy from chapter 4 who almost wet his pants when I took him out for a rappel at Mount Diablo? Well, things sure did change for him. After two years of consistent training, Jim had transformed himself. Forty pounds lighter and working out, he was in fantastic shape. That ninety-foot rappel swung him into a new way of life. Jim redirected his physical lessons to benefit him in his personal and professional life. Not only had he become a skilled rock climber, he also improved himself as a husband, a father, and a person.

After shifting to his "I can do it" mode, Jim was more aware, had better focus, and was much more adept at pulling himself out of the Struggle Syndrome and into the flow of success.

I vividly remember one day when Jim was attempting one of the toughest climbs at Mount Diablo, "the Bolt Ladder," which rises about eighty feet straight up. To complete this route, he had to work his way inch by inch, holding and standing on crimpers, which are basically tiny edges on the smooth face of the rock about as deep as a pinky fingernail is wide. Jim had been working on this route for months. He had pulled off most of the moves, but there was one more, only about ten feet from the final handhold, that he kept falling off whenever he went for it.

As Jim edged his way up to the last part of the climb, I watched and listened as I handled the rope. He was moving well until he got to the place that had been his nemesis. Then he froze. As his body started to shake he looked up, then left and right. Seventy feet below him, I could hear him huffing and puffing like the big bad wolf.

I yelled, "Don't burn out your finger strength! Move and the holds will appear!" Then I heard Jim inhale a big breath and then exhale with purpose. His body stopped trembling. He leaned to the left as he held on with the fingertips of his right hand. Then he lifted his right toe past his right hip and stepped on a little bump on the face of the rock. With powerful grace he rocked over his right foot, pushed up, and wrapped the fingertips of his left hand over the last tiny ledge.

"Ohhh yyyeeesss!" echoed through the canyon as he celebrated the best climb of his life.

Jim knew what to do because he had done the moves so many times before and he had improved his climbing ability through focused practice. He overcame his "obstacle" by drawing on what he knew he could do with the confidence to do it. He remembered to stop, be aware, and resume control.

Jim had gotten himself back into the Zone.

The Zone

Now that, like Jim, you have clarified your vision and you know how to overcome the fears that have been holding you back from your goals, it's time to get into the Zone.

What is the Zone? It's that great "high" you often hear about from athletes who achieve a flow state where their energy is used most effectively and their focus is unwavering. Those who have been there describe an almost mystical experience that results in heightened awareness, increased confidence, total concentration, and struggle-free momentum. Getting into the Zone is a fundamental goal of high achievers and for good reason. When you're in the Zone, the momentum of what you have achieved carries you forward. Your concentration is focused on accomplishing your goal because where you are and what you are doing feels so right.

In contrast, if you're out of the Zone, your mind can drift, diverting attention to irrelevant or even negative thoughts.

In this, and the next two chapters, I'm going to show you how to create and maintain momentum so that you can get into and stay in the Zone. You'll gain new ways to stay focused and effective as you move toward greater success. You'll learn how to keep your attention on what you truly want by using success habits.

It's time for you to enter the Zone.

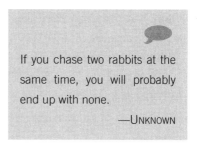

If you chase two rabbits at the same time, you will probably end up with none.

—Unknown

From Inertia to Momentum

In the last chapter you "stepped over the line" from doing what you were doing to what you want to do. Now, using momentum on the goal side of the line, you're going to keep moving toward your intention. This will increase your momentum and get you into and keep you in the Zone.

Webster's dictionary defines momentum as the force possessed by a body in motion. Webster's also defines inertia as "the property of matter which tends to retain its state of rest." An inert object doesn't have the power to move itself.

The laws of inertia and momentum remind me of when I owned an old beat-up Ford with a very weak battery. Luckily this car had a manual transmission so that when the battery couldn't get it started, I could always rely on a rolling jump-start, usually on a straight path. A friend would sit in the driver's seat, put the car in gear, and press down on the clutch pedal. Then I would get behind the car and push it with everything I had.

At first it was brutal to get it moving. By using all my might, the car would slooooowly start to roll. Then it would go faster and faster and I didn't have to work so hard. As the car gained momentum, I could just jog along, pushing it with my fingertips as it kept picking up speed. Finally, I would yell, "Okay," my friend would let out the clutch, the car would start. I'd jump in, and we'd be on our way.

Much the same thing happens when you start progressing toward your goals. Once you begin the process, you create the force of momentum, which, in turn, generates more directed drive. Then, just like my old Ford, your project or task starts picking up speed with greater ease.

Focusing **on your vision helps you clarify where you want to go.** *Staying focused* **gets you there.**

When you stay focused and keep a commitment, you create momentum, and momentum creates momentum. When you do this, you leave struggle behind. You are in the Zone, which leads you to Extreme Success.

I've noticed that when people have a compelling vision for what they want to achieve, often they get all amped up. They want their vision *now* and nothing is going to get in their way. Unfortunately, if you get too worked up on achieving your goal as quickly as possible, there's a good chance you will push yourself right out of the Zone. Am I telling you not to give 100 percent? No way. I just want to remind you that at times other areas of your life are going to ask for 100 percent, too. We've talked about this before. Remember balancing extremes?

You see, if you're not aware of what *really* needs your attention, eventually that area of your life is going to become a crisis situation. Then it doesn't matter how amped up you are, you're going to go into overload and begin to struggle.

If you find yourself frustrated or if you constantly feel like everything is a big "have-to," then reexamine your motivation. If you struggle to reach your goals, then maybe the intention you're trying to achieve doesn't fit with what you really want. Don't "should" on yourself! Being in the Zone is about finding the goals that inspire you and doing what needs to be done—with enthusiasm and commitment.

For instance, if you really hate doing the books for your home-based business when your goal is to expand on it, then hire someone to do them for you and focus on what you love. If you are constantly bothered by managing employees and nothing seems to be working, perhaps you need to do some firing and hiring. If you have been trying to get in shape but keep defeating yourself by dipping into the ice cream shop instead of flexing at the health club, then maybe it's time to hire a personal trainer to put some inspiration and fun into your workouts.

Also be aware of the "buffet syndrome." This happens when you start adding things to your life—a little bit of this and that. You try to learn too much, do too much, help too much, work too much, etc. Things that you actually love begin to fall off your plate. Then you end up with what is just "okay." When you force yourself to try a little of everything, you often miss out on what you really enjoy. And enjoyment is about being in the Zone.

Keeping a wide focus on how you are operating allows you to find your ideal state of mind. It's not about push, push, push. Nor is it about kicking back and "hoping" you'll get the results you desire. Simply put, it's about using your focused effort and effectiveness to get into the Zone that works best for you.

By taking a look at what is available and then choosing what is truly the best for you, you can begin to say no to the things that fill up your time and keep you from living with greater joy and ease.

You don't deserve any special rewards for working really hard and hating the process. The only thing you deserve is a bucket of ice water dumped over your head to wake you up to your life. Remember: Struggle is not noble. Seek joy and ease, and you will find them. Look for the flow and you'll find the Zone.

So how can you find your ideal state of mind and style as you aim toward your goals? Being aware of your challenge-ability balance is one of the keys. If you are setting your goals too low, then you will get bored and lose your focus. If you are setting your goals and expectations

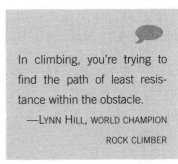

In climbing, you're trying to find the path of least resistance within the obstacle.

—LYNN HILL, WORLD CHAMPION ROCK CLIMBER

too high, you will overload, which can leave you overwhelmed, frustrated, and ineffective.

After Jim's breakthrough climb, I asked him what his "secret" was for continuing to increase his mental and physical momentum.

He told me, "When I climb something too far beyond my ability, I get frustrated. When I climb something too far below my ability, I get bored. When I'm on a climb that takes all of my skill to make it to the top, I get psyched!"

Reality Check

Take a look over your current goals and expectations. How are you setting yourself up? Rate yourself from 1 to 10 based on the following:

1 = You are barely challenging yourself. You are doing just enough to maintain your current condition. Deep down, you know that you're not really taking action toward what you really want in your life. This may be due to fear, laziness, or merely saying to yourself, "I'm going to get to that . . . someday."

10 = You are so challenged that you constantly feel like you are either not doing enough, not capable of achieving the goals you've set, or that you are not putting in enough effort. You get frustrated that you have been falling short of your goals despite giving them 110 percent.

Ultimately, you want to be around a 5. That would mean that you have found a challenge-ability balance where you feel like you are pushing yourself to be the best you can be. It would also mean that you are not banging your head against the wall because you never feel like you have what it takes.

Will there be times when you push yourself beyond a 5? Of course. That's when you'll experience new growth through the failures and lessons, breakdowns and breakthroughs. Just remember to pace yourself. If you are

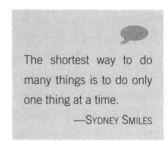

The shortest way to do many things is to do only one thing at a time.
—SYDNEY SMILES

constantly pushing yourself beyond a 5, you'll find yourself burning out and heading into struggle.

Inch by Inch Life's a Cinch

You know what? All of life is a matter of habits, and successful people have successful habits. Those habits help them get in, and stay in, their Zones.

That's what I learned from having ADD, which was like having twenty televisions, all set to different channels, on in the same room and trying to concentrate on every screen simultaneously. For me, staying focused was brutal. Getting into, and staying in, the Zone was nearly impossible!

Eventually I found my remedy through simple structures and strategies. These helped me improve my focus, which led to much greater success both personally and professionally. The best treatment I've seen (when combined with the support and accountability of a coach or a Success Partner) is a set of practical techniques to help stay focused day by day and hour by hour. Bottom line: I developed habits that led to successful outcomes. Each one, in turn, led to the next.

Success Habits award you with a sense of accomplishment and help you work toward your goals. Creating and using Success Habits is one of the best ways I've found to create momentum to move in the direction of your most important goals without getting caught in the Struggle Syndrome.

There are three easy ways to get into the Success Habit practice. I call them the three A's: awareness, action, and accountability. They help you to focus on what you're doing— and staying focused is what being in the Zone is all about.

Awareness. This is where you step back to truly observe your work and your life. You can do this by meditating, journaling, or by talking with a personal coach or your Success Partner. Awareness is where you ask yourself, "What Success Habits could I do on a regular basis that would enhance my life and my success?"

Action. After you figure out what to do, you must do it. You determine which actions to take and how often to do them. Clarifying Success Habits can help you move toward your longer-term goals and a higher-quality life.

Accountability. Often people get clear on what habits could enhance their lives but justify and rationalize all the reasons why they don't do them. This is where accountability pays off big time. You must look at how you will hold yourself accountable to following through on your Success Habits.

Public declaration is a powerful ally here, just as it was when you stepped over the line. Tell your Success Partner what you plan on doing. Ask him or her to hold you accountable to your Success Habits. This may seem like a risky step because it means you are making the commitment to do what is best for you. But that's exactly why you *want* accountability. When you truly desire something (and you are committed to doing what it takes to make it happen) you will *welcome* accountability.

If you're not willing to be held accountable, then you're probably not fully committed to your goal. When you are truly dedicated to achieving a certain outcome, you will *ask* for accountability—no ifs, ands, or buts. Accountability raises the bar. When you do what you say you will do, it raises your self-esteem. You prove to yourself that you can be counted on, that your word matters, and that you keep your agreements.

Also, you need to know that adding more and more things to hold yourself accountable to can dilute your focus and push you into overwhelm. Remember: You can do anything, but you can't do everything (at least, not all at once). When this happens you're in accountability overload. Trim yourself back down to the three most important actions that you can take that will benefit you the most.

When you use the three A's you actually *create* successful habits. Many studies show that if you repeat an action over a twenty-one-day period, it will become a routine.

So if you remind yourself to do something day by day, it can easily become a part of your daily (or weekly) routine. It becomes almost automatic and easy, instead of something you fight to remember and then beat yourself up for forgetting. That means you will be creating momentum and you'll be taking one more step to staying in the Zone of high effectiveness and quality living.

Start by adding the example below onto the Success Partnership Form you learned about in chapter 8, and replace the habits in the example with the habits that *you* want to implement. Begin by coming up with one to three actions that, if done on a regular basis, would contribute to your success and fulfillment.

Each day pull out your current week's SPF and simply circle the day if you completed the habit. This way you'll always be aware of how you're doing. At the end of the week you can share those numbers with your Success Partner.

Some of my most successful clients have told me what a profound impact using Success Habits has made on their achievements and peace of mind. They found that it's the most effective way to track reinforcing behaviors that trigger goal-focusing automatic behaviors.

Example

SUCCESS HABITS FOR THIS WEEK

_____ Call five prospects each weekday

_____ [M T W Th F Sat Sun]

_____ Study for certification exam one hour each morning five times per week

_____ [M T W Th F Sat Sun]

_____ Work out at the club three times per week

_____ [M T W Th F Sat Sun]

RESULTS OF SUCCESS HABITS FROM LAST WEEK

_____ Call five prospects each weekday: 5/5

_____ Study for certification exam one hour each morning five times per week: 4/5

_____ Work out at the club three times per week: 4/3

As you can see, this person made his prospect calls five out of the five days he wanted to, studied for his exam four out of the five days he planned to, and got in an extra workout at the gym over his intended goal. He didn't overextend him-

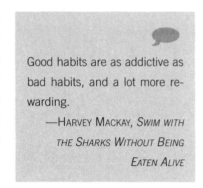

Good habits are as addictive as bad habits, and a lot more rewarding.
—HARVEY MACKAY, *SWIM WITH THE SHARKS WITHOUT BEING EATEN ALIVE*

self, burn out his momentum, or let his attention waiver.

Success Habits = Increased Momentum

My client, Ted, thirty-three, had been a physical therapist for almost ten years when he first hired me to coach him. His main goals were to get new patients and to increase his income. I asked Ted to come up with a list of twenty possible ways to achieve his goals.

Ted arrived at our next coaching session with his list. After acknowledging him for following through, I asked, "Of these twenty ideas, which three do you think would be the most effective?"

Ted chose his top three. Then I said, "Now, of those three, which one would be the easiest to implement?"

After looking at his choices for a little while, Ted told me that he had lots of friends who were willing to refer business to him, but he had been slacking off when it came to calling them. Ted wanted to build his physical therapy business, but he was overwhelmed with all the other stuff he had to do.

He said, "If I were to just follow up with a couple of my current patients each day, I'm sure it would stir up new business for me. I could see how my patients are doing and remind them that I am committed to helping them stay healthy. I would think that with that type of service and care, they would want to refer their friends and families to my office."

Ted asked me to hold him accountable each week to following his new Success Habit. He contacted one patient a day, and the results were outstanding! Ted's patient base began to grow almost every week through referrals. Since then, Ted has added two more Success Habits to his life: walking three times per week and sending a card to a friend or family member every week saying what he appreciates about them. His business is more profitable and his life is more balanced and fulfilling.

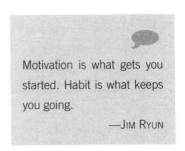

Motivation is what gets you started. Habit is what keeps you going.

—Jim Ryun

Keepers: Thoughts to Remember

- Getting into the Zone is a fundamental goal of high achievers. When you're in the Zone, the momentum of what you have achieved carries you forward.

- *Focusing* on your vision helps you clarify where you want to go. *Staying focused* gets you there.

- When you stay focused and keep a commitment, you create momentum, and momentum creates momentum. When you do this, you leave struggle behind. You are in the Zone, which leads you to Extreme Success.

- If you find yourself frustrated or if you constantly feel like everything is a big "have-to," then reexamine your motivation. If you struggle to reach your goals, then maybe the intention you're trying to achieve doesn't fit with what you really want.

➤ Be aware of the "buffet syndrome," that is, putting too many different things on your plate at the same time.

➤ Be aware of your challenge-ability balance. If you are setting your goals too low, you will get bored and lose your focus. If you are setting your goals too high, you will be frustrated and ineffective.

➤ Success Habits are a great way to create ongoing momentum.

➤ To establish Success Habits use the three A's: awareness, action, and accountability.

➤ Remember that inch by inch, life's a cinch (but yard by yard, life is hard!)

Action Idea #27: Make a Success Habit

Think of one habit, however small, that would add to your success if you did it on a daily basis. Make a commitment to yourself to do it this week. If you really want to improve the results of this strategy, track your Success Habit on your Success Partnership Form (see chapter 8) and ask your partner to hold you accountable. Tell your partner that at the end of the week, you will let him or her know how many times you followed through on your habit. Use the power of partnership and public declaration to increase your chance of success. Enjoy the process!

17

Re-Zoning Takes Extreme Energy

When walking, walk; when eating, eat.

—Zen maxim

In rock climbing there is usually a certain line or route you must follow to reach the top of the cliff. If you don't stay aware and you get off route, it takes a lot of energy to find the route again and climb back over to it. And the farther you get from the line, the more effort you use getting back on route.

It's the same when you fall out of the Zone. This happens when you lose focus on what really matters to you. As a result, you land in a rut that gets deeper and deeper the longer you are in it. And the farther you fall out of the Zone, the harder it is to return to it.

For example, imagine that one of your Success Habits is to reply to your E-mails at the end of each day. This puts you in the Zone because you feel good accomplishing something you want to do. But let's say that for a couple of days you don't "feel like" doing it so you avoid it. Several days later, you realize that you are faced with "inbox overload." You say to yourself, "Oh man! I have so many E-mails to return and I just don't have the time today." So you skip it a few more days. By the end of just one week, you are overwhelmed.

You just fell out of your Work Zone and it's going to take a lot of extra effort to get back into it. You could just delete all the E-mails and hope that none of them were critical to your career. Or you could stay late after work for a few days and get caught up. Either way, falling out of the Zone lands you smack dab in the Struggle Syndrome.

I've seen this happen with people who pack on pounds over the holidays. They avoid dealing with the problem and—no surprise—it gets worse and worse. Frustrated, they obsess about their problem while feeling angry with themselves (and sometimes others). Often they feel like just giving up.

Now I know that holidays are eating fests and most of us like to indulge (me too!). So to make sure that my clients don't fall out of their Fitness Zone, here's what I do. After the holidays I ask them how satisfied they are with their health and fitness. Sure, some gain weight. However—and this is the key point—most are not too stressed about it because they know it is still manageable. We set up a simple first step to get them back in the Zone of healthy eating and exercise again. That's all it takes. Because I am their Success Partner, I have them check in on how they are feeling and how content they are. We come up with a plan and set up accountability for it. It works!

You and your Success Partner can do the same for each other. (I do with mine.)

The Zone Is a State of Mind

Being aware of how you are operating and feeling is vital. Maybe you've said to yourself, "This is my new commitment

and I'm going to follow through on it." Then you end up not
following through and, in a sense, you break that original
agreement with yourself and slip out of the Zone.

If you've let this happen you probably know how lousy
that feels. When you break an agreement with yourself, you
end up sending a message to your inner self that you can't be
counted on or that you don't have what it takes to be successful. And that is just not true!

I ask my clients to clarify if the action they say they are going to take is a goal or an agreement. Here is how I define the
difference. A goal is something you're shooting for, just like
an archery target. You set up the goal (target) to give yourself
something to aim toward. If you don't hit the bull's-eye at
least you know you have a direction. You can keep practicing
until you find your best shooting style.

An agreement is a promise. When you make an agreement with yourself or with another person it means you are
going to do your very best to make it happen.

If one of my clients says, "I will finish that report by Wednes-
day," I'll ask, "Is that a goal or an agreement?" This allows both
of us to know how important this action really is. If my client
says, "It's an agreement," she knows that I won't let it slide by if
she doesn't follow through. I'm going to really challenge her to
look at what got in the way of her completing it.

If my client says, "It's a goal," she knows that if she doesn't
follow through, I'll say something like, "Okay, do you want
to carry that action forward or is it not that important?" This
allows my client to stay clear and in action on what really
matters. It also allows me to know when to be tough and
when to take it easier with accountability.

What type of message do you send yourself? Can you say,
"I do what I say I will do"? Or do you find yourself saying
stuff like, "I just don't have the time to do all this," or "I tried

to do it, but my plate is too full," or "I wanted to achieve this, but 'they' didn't support me."

That's why working with a Success Partner is so important. He or she will help you define what you want and help you get back to it—and the Zone—ASAP.

The Partnership Zone

When I was training for a bodybuilding contest, there would be days where I had no desire to work out. Tired and irritated, I was far from being in the Zone. It was on those days that my training partner brought me back. He would say something like, "Oh, you're not really in the mood to train today? Well, *I'm* psyched. I'm gonna show you what time it is, bud, so you better wake up!" That would get me going and we'd end up having a terrific workout. On other days, when my training partner was less than excited to have a kick-butt workout, I'd say something similar to get him going.

It's like geese flying in formation. Some geese take the lead and the others follow behind in their slipstream. Then, when the front geese tire out, their buddies come up from behind and take the lead. It's all about using the power of partnership to stay in the Zone.

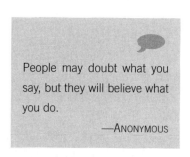

People may doubt what you say, but they will believe what you do.

—ANONYMOUS

If You Make It, Keep It

A while ago, one of my coaching clients started breaking his promises with me shortly after he began work on a large project. Barry, forty-seven, who is the vice president of a telecommunications company, would come up with a great idea and say, "I'm going to complete this by next week." A week later, he would say, "I didn't get to it." Not only was he breaking his promise with me, he was also letting himself down. He would get clarity on how he could improve his work and his life, but then he would flake on keeping his commitments.

I asked Barry where else he was making and breaking promises. *That* hit home. After a moment of silence, Barry said, "With my boss, my wife, my kids . . . wow, I'm breaking promises all over the place!" I asked him about recent pledges he had broken. He said, "I told my boss that I'd have a report to him by the end of the day and I didn't get it to him until two days later. I told my wife that I would be home by six and then I got home at nine. I told my kids that I would go on a bike ride with them on the weekend and then I ended up spending the time on a work project. This is not good!"

Barry could see that his behavior was having a negative impact on his relationships, so I gave him the following challenge: "For one month I challenge you to not make any promises that you can't keep and to honor all the promises you make." Barry agreed.

Several weeks later Barry was very happy that he had taken on that challenge. His relationships with his boss, his wife, and his kids had improved dramatically. What Barry has noticed the most, though, is how much better he feels about himself.

So the bottom line is that when we overextend ourselves and make promises we can't keep, it pushes us out of the

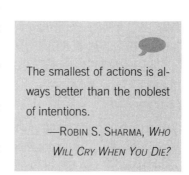

The smallest of actions is always better than the noblest of intentions.

—ROBIN S. SHARMA, *WHO WILL CRY WHEN YOU DIE?*

Zone. When we set boundaries and maintain a reserve of time in which to achieve what we commit to, it is much easier to stay in the Zone and stay out of feeling overwhelmed and frustrated.

A Fine Way to Get Motivated

Jeff, twenty-six, had a goal to exercise three times per week. He said that when he worked out he felt better and more energetic. His day was more fulfilling, too. This was a Zone pattern if there ever was one. The problem was that Jeff stopped working out! His job as a financial planner took up much of his time, and he always seemed to have an excuse for not making it to the health club. I could sense the frustration in his voice during our coaching sessions whenever he told me that another week went by without a workout.

I asked Jeff the reasons he wanted to work out. He gave me a list of all the reasons and benefits and then said, "I just don't seem to have the discipline in the moment. When I have the chance to go to the gym, I usually find something else to do, like call a couple clients or organize my office."

"What association or organization has a mission that you don't believe in?" I asked. He named one. "Okay, Jeff, let's set up a fine. If you don't get three workouts in by next week's coaching session, will you mail a check to that organization for five hundred dollars?"

There was silence on the other end of the phone. He knew this was not only a test to see how committed he was to exercising, but also a way to challenge him to take action on a goal that had been eluding him for months.

Finally, Jeff said, "Yes, I accept that challenge." The next week he came to his coaching call excited and inspired. He had gotten in three great workouts and felt energized! The dare worked. He asked to keep the same challenge going for the next week, then the next week, and so on. The fine was the push Jeff needed. The momentum he created by developing the habit of three workouts per week continued, and after a few weeks he didn't even need the fine anymore (though he chose to keep it just in case). Jeff was back in the Zone.

Excuses, Excuses

People often hold themselves accountable to the wrong things. We harbor a strong desire to do what is easiest instead of what is most essential. For instance, we justify not working on an important project because we have too many errands to get done. This is a surefire way to tumble out of the Zone and into the Struggle Syndrome.

This is why you can't allow your weekly goals (those things you are shooting toward) to become excuses for not doing what is most crucial (your agreements). By determining ahead of time what is an agreement and what is a goal, you will have a much better chance of doing what really matters by the week's end.

Getting Back into the Zone

If you find yourself out of the Zone, here are some tips you can use in the moment to get back into it with greater ease.

1. Shift your attention to your breathing. When you become stressed, anxious, angry, or afraid, your breathing speeds up

and gets shallow. Slow down your breathing. Inhale deeply through your nose and then exhale through your mouth. Remember to do this when you need that precious oxygen the most.

2. Place your hand on your "power center." This place varies from person to person. For some it's their heart, for others it's their solar plexus (that soft spot just below your sternum). Some folks hold their power in their throat, upper chest, or pelvis. To find your power center, close your eyes and feel where you notice the greatest inner strength in your body. Put your hand there and breathe. You'll feel what I'm talking about. When you put your hand over your power center you can shift your attention there and feel your energy rise. Allow that energy to flow throughout your body, and you will gracefully shift into grounded strength and awareness.

3. Have a mantra that grounds you. For example, "Stop, be aware, resume control" has worked well for me. I also use two simple words—"breathe Rich." My clients have told me about other re-Zoning mantras that work well for them: "The power is in my heart," "All is well, all is well," and "Let go and let God."

These three techniques can help you return to the Zone. You can use one or all of them. The key is to practice them on a regular basis. Maybe put a sticky note in a prominent place to remind you. You could also use the hourly chime on your watch, your personal digital assistant, or on your computer to remind you to check in and see how you're feeling. Again, awareness and mindfulness are vital to being in the Zone. These techniques can help you avoid "checking out."

You will be in the moment more often, which will help you arrive at the future you most desire.

Falling out of the Zone happens. Just remember that you *can* get back into it. Breathe, center yourself, and focus on what really matters—and you'll find your way back, without struggle.

Keepers: Thoughts to Remember

➤ When you lose focus on what really matters, you can fall out of the Zone. And the farther you are out of the Zone, the harder it is to return to it.

➤ Being aware of how you are operating and feeling is vital to staying in the Zone.

➤ Asking your Success Partner to fine you if you don't follow through on an agreement can be the jump-start that pushes you into action. Remember to reward yourself after you take action.

➤ Make only those promises that you can keep.

➤ Keeping agreements with yourself is also vital to staying in the Zone.

➤ Clarify if the action you say you are going to take is a goal or an agreement. A goal is something you're just shooting for. An agreement is a promise you are going to do your best to make happen.

➤ By determining ahead of time what is an agreement and what is a goal you will know what really matters.

➤ When you set boundaries and maintain a reserve of time in which to achieve what you commit to, it is much easier to stay in the Zone.

➤ If you find yourself out of the Zone, here is a ritual you can use in the moment to get back into the Zone with greater ease: Shift your attention to your breathing, place your hand on your "power center," have a mantra that grounds you.

Action Idea #28: Commit to Keeping Your Promises

Make a personal commitment for the rest of this month (or longer) to make only promises that you can keep and to keep all the promises that you make. Before you make any promises, ask yourself if you are definitely going to follow through 100 percent. Then, write down any of the promises that you make and share this information with your Success Partner. Ask your Success Partner to check in with you each week on how you're doing with those promises.

Action Idea #29: Create Rituals

Rituals are very helpful to help keep you in the Zone. Going for a walk first thing in the morning, clearing your desk at the end of each workday, checking your voice mail on a regular schedule, meeting with employees at the same time each day (or week) to find out how they are doing and to coach them for greater effectiveness—these are just a few things you can do. Take a look at your rituals and see what has worked for you. Also take a look at where you might be able to follow some new rituals to help you stay focused and in the Zone.

Finally, write down one daily ritual that might add to your energy and fulfillment and put it into action. Begin today and notice how the power of one simple ritual can add to your happiness and peace of mind. It can help you stay in the Zone more often now and in the years to come.

Action Idea #30: Make It Real

Write down one thing that you have not done, or that you're not doing on a consistent basis, that would help you get back into the Zone.

Asking your Success Partner to fine you if you don't follow through may provide the jump-start that pushes you into action. Decide what type of fine would motivate you to follow through on your positive habit or action. Also, what would be your reward after you complete this challenge? If you earn your reward, take it. Don't diminish your success by thinking that you don't deserve it. Celebrate! Notice what worked for you to keep your commitment.

But don't diminish the consequence of not keeping your agreement by not following through with your agreed upon fine. Do it. Make it real. Show yourself that you mean business and promise, "I'm not going to let that happen again."

Use the challenge of a fine with your Success Partner and watch how you both get into and stay in the Zone.

18

Do Today What Brings Joy Tomorrow

Commitment leads to action, and action brings your dream closer.
—Marcia Wieder, *Making Your Dreams Come True*

Years ago I learned a philosophy from one of my mentors that has helped me feel better about myself, and my life, day after day. I want to share it because I believe it will do the same for you.

The philosophy is this: Do today what brings joy tomorrow.

Using this approach allows you to make intelligent choices instead of those that just satisfy a need in the moment. It will help keep you in the Zone of happiness and fulfillment day after day.

Here's an example. If I thought, Hmm, I don't feel like working this morning. I think I'll go watch TV, it might feel good as I'm doing it. But there is a strong chance that the next day I'd regret it because I missed a chance to work in the Zone.

Now, if I asked myself, Will doing that bring me joy tomorrow? I might say, No, I'm just being lazy. I'll feel best if I do some work and *then* watch TV later. Or I might say, Yes, I feel burned out right now. I honestly think getting away from my office is the best thing for me right now. That way tomorrow I'll come back recharged and ready to go.

By looking at things this way, you filter your choices through what is best for you in the short term *and* in the long term. This is a proactive way to handle your decisions. It's about taking in the big picture and living your life with awareness and mindfulness. You're able to make choices that are truly the best for you on a deeper level.

This strategy adds to your life, allowing you to experience more joy more often. When you do today what brings joy tomorrow, you will sustain your bliss and send a powerful message to yourself. You keep your word. You walk your talk. You know how to get in, and stay in, the Zone.

In the Zone your senses expand and intuition strengthens, allowing you to see and seize new opportunities. The chances of creating intentional luck rise extraordinarily. You see opportunities that you are prepared for and you access the courage to act on them. A more fulfilling life is yours.

Think about it. If you did the things yesterday that would bring you joy today you'd feel pretty good right now, wouldn't you? So why not start applying this principle right now? You will feel better, enjoy the moment, and make progress toward achieving your visions and goals. You'll be in the Zone, today and always.

Remember: You can control your activities, not your outcomes. As one of my climbing guides told me, "It's not just about reaching the summit. You must also enjoy the climb."

One Simple Ritual

Recently my wife and I enjoyed a wonderful vacation visiting our family and friends on the East Coast. However, I allowed myself to let go of my usual rituals such as getting up early in the morning, going for a daily walk, practicing yoga, and writing. For a while, it felt nice to wake up and be "lazy" as I let the day steer me wherever it wanted to. But after a few days I began to feel lethargic, unhealthy, and "numb."

Thank goodness, I realized something needed to change. I asked myself, What simple ritual could I bring back that might help me feel better tomorrow? I decided to do a short stretching and deep-breathing program right after I woke up. The first day I did this (within two minutes of getting up) I felt great! My body tingled with energy and I could feel every cell fill with oxygen. I made a promise to myself that I would bring this one easy routine into my vacations from that point on—beginning with the very next day.

Reality Check

Here are a few questions you can ask yourself that may give you more clarity on deciding what to do today to bring joy tomorrow. The more questions that you answer yes to the better the chance is that your choice will be the right one.

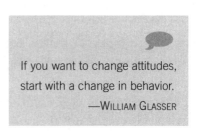

If you want to change attitudes, start with a change in behavior.
—WILLIAM GLASSER

➤ Does this move me closer to my long-term vision?

➤ Does this feel like a "want-to" instead of a "have-to"?

➤ When I wake up tomorrow morning, will I be happy that I made this choice?

➤ Is this worth the cost of not doing my other options today?

➤ Does my intuition (inner wisdom) say it's a good idea?

Who's Kidding Whom?

"I don't know what I want to focus on this session. I seem to be on track with all my goals," Dave said as we began our coaching session. He had originally hired me as his coach to focus on building his computer consulting business. Dave was right; his life was working very well. In just over six months he had raised his profits by almost 30 percent, dropped twelve pounds, and was finally taking weekends off to spend time with his wife.

It appeared that Dave had it all together, so I said to him, "I want you to wait until you're ready to answer a question: Are you willing to be one hundred percent honest with yourself?"

He nodded.

"Where in your life might you be kidding yourself?" I questioned.

After what seemed like a full minute, Dave mumbled, "I haven't done anything for my spiritual life in almost three years." Not coincidentally, Dave had started his business about three years before. He said that he was so busy and tired in those years that he decided to put his religious practices "on hold for a little while."

"Is it time for you to do something about that?" I asked. After some discussion, Dave agreed to take a twenty-four-hour spiritual retreat on his own, without his cell phone, laptop, or PalmPilot. He wanted to unplug from the day-to-day whirlwind that had been tugging him away from his soul nourishment. When we were wrapping up our coaching session, Dave said to me, "How did you know I had been kidding myself about this?"

"I had no idea," I replied. "But *you* did."

Focus on the process of going for your goals, allow obstacles to be experiences to learn from, and trust that where you are is a step on the way to the summit. When you do this, you will be able to flow through your life with less effort and struggle. You will experience more joy and ease. You will live in the Zone.

Design Your Ideal Day

Remember when we talked about recording a future ideal day on audiotape? Well, this is a similar exercise, but its focus is on today. Think about what your ideal day would look like. You might have several, including a day spent on vacation, on a weekend, or at work.

You don't know exactly how things are going to turn out, but you do give yourself an idea of what you're shooting for. From there you get a much better idea of where you need to put attention and which things are going well.

Here are some questions that can help you envision your ideal day. I suggest closing your eyes first and imagining it. Then write down what you see. You can also close your eyes after you ask yourself each of the following questions and discover what you see. Then write your answers down for your future reference.

Type of ideal day? (i.e., workday, vacation day, weekend day)

➤ How would you begin your day?

➤ What would you be doing in the late morning?

➤ What would you be doing in the afternoon?

➤ What would you be doing in the early evening?

➤ What would you be doing in the late evening?

➤ What would make this an ideal day?

➤ What did you learn from this exercise?

➤ What are your next steps?

Some clients have done this exercise by journaling a few paragraphs of their ideal day. Other clients have come up with an actual schedule with times when they would do different activities. You can do either or both. It helps to see what you want in order to have what you see.

Keepers: Thoughts to Remember

➤ If your philosophy is "Do today what brings joy tomorrow," you will make intelligent choices instead of those that just satisfy a need in the moment. You will stay in the Zone of happiness and fulfillment day after day.

➤ Remember that you can control your activities, not your outcomes.

➡ Focus on the process of going for your goals, allow obstacles to be experiences to learn from, and trust that where you are is a step on the way to the summit.

➡ Map out your ideal day. You might have several different kinds of days, including one spent on vacation, during a weekend, or at work. This will help you get clear on how to actually have these days happen. It helps to see what you want in order to have what you see.

Action Idea #31: Think Long Term

For one week practice "Do Today What Brings Joy Tomorrow." Give deliberate thought to how you are living. Throughout each day, ask yourself questions such as:

➡ Is what I'm doing now also going to bring me joy tomorrow?

➡ Will planning what I want to do right now add to my overall quality of life?

➡ Does this move me closer to my long-term vision?

➡ Does this feel like a "want-to" or a "have-to"?

➡ Is what I am doing or about to do something I will regret tomorrow?

➡ What could I do now that would really have me feeling great when I wake up in the morning?

➡ Is this worth the cost of not doing my other options today?

Pay attention to how this works for you. Each day record how you felt, what you learned, and what you will do with this knowledge. This one exercise can dramatically affect your fulfillment and peace of mind.

After applying this philosophy for one week, write down which choices you made that contributed to your quality of life.

Action Idea #32: Stop Kidding Yourself

Invest the next few minutes at your keyboard or in a journal and answer the question: Where in my life might I be kidding myself? Pause for a moment now and really check in with yourself. Be 100 percent honest. Look deep inside yourself and you will find the answer. Once you have your answer, you'll know what to do next. My challenge to you is to do something about it by the end of this week. As always, I wish you the best.

PART 7

Enjoy the High!

19

---->

In a Moment, It Could Happen

Attitude is the reflection of a person, and our world mirrors our attitude.

—Earl Nightingale

I drove out to the hills, pulled on my backpack full of climbing gear, and began my hike. I was told it was only about a mile from the parking lot to the cliffs, so I took off at a quick pace. I also wanted to get in as much climbing as possible, and I had told my friends Jim and Tresa that I would meet them at the cliffs.

After hiking a windy, inclining trail for over half an hour I looked ahead and saw that the trail went over the top of a ridge. I thought to myself, The cliffs must be on the other side.

As I approached the crest of the well-worn trail, huffing and puffing, I imagined that I'd see my climbing partners already working on a route. I envisioned Jim belaying as Tresa made her way toward the top of a cliff.

But that's not what I saw. Immediately my thoughts changed to: Oh no, I might be on the wrong trail. Still, I decided to keep up the pace and hike to the next ridge, where I thought that I would see my friends. One hundred feet to go, fifty feet, twenty feet, almost there . . . "Not again!"

I repeated this scenario several times. A one-mile hike had turned into a three-mile trek—with lots of hills! My pack was getting heavier and my legs were starting to feel like well-cooked noodles. I began to think that I'd never reach my destination.

Finally, I made it to the top of another ridge and my vision became a reality. Tresa was near the top of a climb while Jim belayed her from below. I let out a big "Yes!" and joined them for some extreme fun.

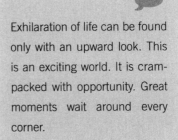

Exhilaration of life can be found only with an upward look. This is an exciting world. It is cram-packed with opportunity. Great moments wait around every corner.

—Richard M. DeVos

It Only Takes a Moment

Have you ever thought that your goal was "just around the corner" until you discovered that it was much farther than you had hoped? Many people give up at the first frustration and say something like, "Well, I guess it's just not meant for me."

I've heard lots of people complain about what they lack. They whine about how other people bring them down or how messed up the world is. Keeping your focus on what you don't have or complaining about others not being the way you want them to be is a one-way path to the Struggle Syndrome. Accepting responsibility for your own success, and trusting that in a moment you can shift your perspective to gratefulness and abundance can bring you back to the road to fulfillment.

If you think that one of your goals seems to be taking longer than you had anticipated, take a look at how you are moving toward it. Are you on the right path? Do you really want to make this dream a reality? Is there someone who could join you on the journey and make it more enjoyable?

If you decide that this goal is truly an important one for you, then say to yourself, "It might be just around the corner. I'm continuing on the path and I'm enjoying the beautiful scenes along the way. In a moment, it could happen."

If you've been working on a goal that seems to keep getting farther and farther away, I want to encourage you: Stay on the path a little longer. Your attitude is key. An occasional glance toward the summit will keep your intention in mind. But don't forget to take in the many beautiful scenes along the way. Shifting your perspective to what you have in your life, as opposed to getting so focused on what you want, can improve your attitude, increase your inspiration, and add to your fulfillment. Then, you never know when you'll come over the crest and your goal will be just a few steps away. It could happen at any moment.

A breakthrough may be just around the corner for you— "just like that"—*if* you believe it. If you think that, for you, success has to be a struggle, then I'm asking you to turn that belief around 180 degrees and "try on" the viewpoint that

In a moment we could change.
—ED ROLAND OF COLLECTIVE SOUL, "IN A MOMENT"

success can be easy, that you can have what you want with joy and ease. In a moment you could:

➤ meet the person who will help catapult you toward your goals;

➤ realize that success does not have to be a struggle;

➤ muster the courage to go for what you want with 100 percent intention and belief.

Do a 180

Not too long ago, in a workshop I was facilitating, we were doing the Trust Fall. This is an event where each participant has the chance to really test his or her views on support.

One participant climbs up onto a platform that's about six feet above the ground. This person stands, facing backward. Ten other participants line up in two facing rows beneath the platform. Holding out their hands, they create a safety "net" that the participant on the platform will fall onto.

After several successful "falls" I asked Marlene to climb up next. I stood on the platform with her as the rest of the group lined up to catch her. Despite her efforts to look like she had it all together, Marlene's eyes filled with tears as her body trembled.

"What is this fall about for you, Marlene?" I asked.

"I don't know. I'm just scared. I don't know why I'm so emotional about this."

"What do you want right now?"

"I want to get down," she blurted out. "I don't want to do this."

"Okay. You know that you don't *have* to do this. It's your choice. But first let me ask: What is your fear telling you right now?"

"My fear is telling me that they are going to drop me."

"Well, no wonder you're scared. That's pretty hard ground down there. I wouldn't want to fall back if my team was going to drop me either." Then I stood close so that my face was only a few inches from hers. I whispered, "Do you *ever* let people be there for you?"

Marlene started to gasp and tears flowed down her cheeks. "No," she admitted. "I feel like I'm always on my own and nobody really cares."

"Then I want you to do a one-eighty. Turn your body around and face the opposite direction."

Marlene slowly shuffled herself around until she was looking down at her team.

"What do you see?" I asked.

"I see a bunch of great people with their arms out ready to catch me."

"Ask them if they care."

"Do you care?" Marlene asked.

The group responded with a resounding "Yes!"

"There you have it, Marlene. These people *want* to support you. They want to be there for you. So now what do you want?" I asked.

"I want to do it, but I don't know if I can."

Then someone from the group spoke. "Marlene, you can do it. C'mon, we'll be here!"

At that moment something happened to Marlene. She turned around again so her back was to the group. This time she stood taller. As she looked intensely into my eyes, she whispered, "I can do this!"

"Yes, you can. Ask your team if they are ready to catch you."

Marlene shouted, "Hey, you guys, are you ready?"

Everyone responded, "Yes, we're ready!"

Marlene took in a deep breath and said, "Falling!" With her arms crossed on her chest and her body as straight as a board, I heard her gasp. And then she fell, eyes squeezed shut, into the waiting arms of her supporters.

"Keep holding her," I instructed. The team held Marlene horizontally as tears of relief and joy spilled from her eyes. After several seconds she opened her eyes and looked around at the people holding her. Then she broke into a laugh that sounded like waves of ecstasy. The whole group laughed with her. Then I said, "Okay, please lower her to her feet."

When we debriefed this exercise Marlene said, "I don't know why, but for as long as I can remember I've always had a trust issue. I've tried to do everything on my own because I thought people either didn't want to help me or because I thought if I *did* get help I'd be let down. In that exercise, I felt the same way when I stepped up on the platform. Then something shifted inside me. When I looked down and saw all of you standing there, I knew you were there for me. It was like I changed my old beliefs at that moment. When I was lying in your arms I felt like a new person. I felt supported but strong at the same time. That was a completely new feeling for me."

In a moment Marlene changed her perspective. She not only did a 180-degree turn with her body, she did the same with her mind. I've seen similar "miracles" happen with other people, too. You can do the same thing yourself.

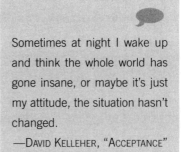

Sometimes at night I wake up and think the whole world has gone insane, or maybe it's just my attitude, the situation hasn't changed.

—DAVID KELLEHER, "ACCEPTANCE"

Take a Quick Self-test

Right now, look in front of you for everything that is blue. Really look carefully and notice everything that is blue. Got it? C'mon, if you haven't done it, do it now, then resume reading this.

Okay, now turn around 180 degrees from where you were looking. Think about all the things that were red. Now, turn back again and look for anything that is red. Interesting, huh? Did you see more things that were red than when you were looking for blue? I bet you did.

You see, when you are stuck in one perspective, you limit your possibilities. When you look with a new perspective, you often see what you had not noticed before but was always there.

By "trying on" new perspectives, you have a much better chance of noticing the opportunities around you. It can happen in just a moment.

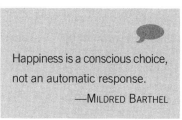

Happiness is a conscious choice, not an automatic response.
—MILDRED BARTHEL

It's Great to Be Grateful

My plane was soaring about halfway between Dallas and San Francisco. I had just given a speech and was returning home on an afternoon flight. The man sitting next to me must have been in his nineties. He had a blanket spread out over his legs and he was reading a book.

When the flight attendants brought our lunches, I ripped off the cover of mine, grabbed my fork, and prepared to scarf down my meal. Out of the corner of my eye, I noticed that the older gentleman was not eating. In fact, he was motionless. His eyes were closed and his hands were folded. Then he smiled, gave a small nod, opened his eyes, and began to eat.

At that moment I realized how often I hadn't taken the

time to give thanks. In my flurry of daily activity I was letting myself forget about all the wonderful things to be grateful for. I made a promise to myself that I would pause before each meal and give myself a moment to give thanks.

By practicing awareness and gratefulness, you will notice more of the opportunities and joys and gifts around you. This is one of the most powerful ways to open up to new perspectives.

It's been over a year since I made that promise, and I want you to know how valuable it has been. Every day I become more and more aware of the friendship, love, abundance, and joy that are around me. And I'll tell you: This perspective sure makes me happy—moment by moment.

Keepers: Thoughts to Remember

➤ Accepting responsibility for your own success, and trusting that in a moment you can shift your perspective to gratitude and abundance can put you on the road to fulfillment.

➤ If you focus on what you don't have, you will end up on a one-way path to the Struggle Syndrome.

➤ When you are stuck in one perspective, you limit your possibilities. When you look with a new perspective, you often see what was always there but you had not noticed before.

➤ By "trying on" new perspectives, you have a much better chance of noticing the opportunities around you.

➤ Being aware and grateful will help you notice more of the opportunities and joys and gifts around you.

Action Idea #33: Be Grateful

For the next seven days practice gratefulness. Come up with a routine (such as a moment of silence, thanks, or prayer before each meal) that will remind you to pause, reflect, and give thanks for all that you have in your life. After seven days, notice the benefits you are receiving from this ritual. You will not only feel better, most likely you will see new opportunities that you had not seen before. If you like the way you're feeling, then by all means, keep on giving thanks.

20

---→

Fly High, See More

An open mind collects more riches than an open purse.

—Anonymous

You are prepared for the next step on your incredible journey. If you want to live out a dream, whether it's starting your own business, moving to the top of your company, traveling around the world, increasing your income, getting into great physical shape, improving your personal life, or stepping beyond the apparent limits of your day-to-day life—even all of the above—Extreme Success can be yours. The strategies you need are in your hands.

You also possess another powerful asset: self-knowledge. You know what you have accomplished so far. And now you know what you are capable of doing.

Because you strive to get the most out of life, you took the time to learn how to create opportunity as well as luck.

You own the information that can break you free from struggle. You know how to:

➤ free yourself from the limiting perspectives of the past so that you are ready to act on the best opportunities now and in the future;

➤ seek balance in all areas of your life;

➤ find the right partners and get the help you need;

➤ create a compelling vision of where you are going;

➤ focus your attention on your intention;

➤ take risks and overcome the fear factor;

➤ maintain momentum by getting in and staying in the Zone of high effectiveness;

➤ be ready to face future challenges and opportunities with greater joy, effectiveness, and ease.

I can't wait to hear about your journey, where it will take you, and what you will achieve. Please let me know about it, because I want to tell others about it.

Just like Tamara, Michael, Jim, Christine, Shane, Paul, and Marlene, you are about to create your own success story. You, too, can push your limits, reach your highest goals, and experience more joy.

Ultimately, as you revel in your ability to build on past achievements, you're going to ride the wave of astonishing exhilaration that flows from attaining what you really want. As you do so, you are going to appreciate something pretty amazing: the exceptional person you already are and the extraordinary person you are going to become.

Mirror, Mirror

What would you like to acknowledge yourself for? Come on, don't skip this question. Stop. Think about this. So often people just shrug off their accomplishments. That's why I ask my clients to do the Mirror Exercise.

I'd like you to do it, too. Ready? Stand in front of a mirror and gaze deeply into your eyes. Now acknowledge yourself for who you are and what you have done. State the things you're proud of out loud; really honor your achievements. Feels good, doesn't it?

Hold on—you're not done yet! I understand that the following might be awkward, but here's what I want you to do.

Keep looking in the mirror and say out loud, "I love you." (Yeah, I bet you're probably thinking, "Now I *know* this guy is from Northern California!")

I've had clients tell me that they immediately turned away. Some laughed. A few cried. The folks who actually allowed themselves to experience this kind of deep self-validation felt a new and profound sense of inner peace and confidence.

And that makes sense. When you develop yourself, and your character, you acquire a wide-angle view of your achievements while focusing on their source.

When you walk your talk, honor agreements with yourself, and feel proud of the unique per-

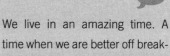

We live in an amazing time. A time when we are better off breaking the rules than keeping them. . . . So many of the rules you live by are perceived expectations you have placed on yourself. Get out and be free. You hold the key to your own best life.

—LAURA BERMAN FORTGANG, *LIVING YOUR BEST LIFE*

son that you are, you will be able to do the Mirror Exercise with ease. It will fuel you. By loving who you are—and the person you are evolving into—your ability to achieve Extreme Success increases exponentially.

Well, sure. You are developing *yourself,* and when that happens success develops with you. The only way to really be successful is to work from the inside—that means *you*—out. Trying to do it the other way around is a time-tested formula for disappointment.

It's Time to Boldly Go Where You Have Never Gone Before

Imagine that you are standing in a small airport. As you look around, you notice that this is actually a skydiving "drop zone." You watch as jumpers gracefully glide toward earth under their multicolored canopies.

Then you hear me say, "Great to see you! Ready to go big?" I hand you a parachute, goggles, and a helmet before we board a small airplane. As the plane takes off, you look around. The other skydivers are excited and smiling. Their energy is so positive and upbeat that it's intoxicating. You feel connected to both the community of jumpers and the thrill you are going to share.

As the plane climbs higher and the view becomes wider, you are aware of the extensive expanse that is available to you. Being so high up gives you a whole new perspective about what "the world is your oyster" really means. The planet below you is filled with wonderful things to learn and do and experience. That world contains many pearls waiting for you to discover them.

You think to yourself, I'm up here because I decided to

push my limits. I want to succeed at something new. I want to develop more of my inner strength to go after anything I desire in my life.

Suddenly, someone yells out, "Fourteen thousand feet! It's time to skydive!" Your adrenaline kicks in with a familiar exhilarating boost.

But then your Protector makes itself heard by declaring inside your head, "No way. I won't let you do this!"

In response, you simply close your eyes and the two of you have a little "talk." Comforted, your Protector quiets down.

A moment later you ask me the procedure to follow in the air and ask me to check out your rig to make sure everything is in place. We review what you need to do and then I check your pack.

"Everything looks great," I reply as I give you a firm pat on the back.

Then someone opens the plane door and the cool wind howls its way in. Four skydivers step to the door, look at each other, and yell out, "Ready . . . set . . . go!" and leap out of the plane.

I grab your arm and peer in your eyes.

"Are you ready to skydive?" I shout over the roar of the wind and the engines.

You nod affirmatively because you feel an amazing confidence that everything is going to be just fine. As your heartbeat seems to pulse throughout your body you shout out, "Ready!"

We jump out of the plane into one of the most exciting experiences of your life. I'm holding on to you as we fall, straight down, belly first at 120 miles per hour. You realize how reassuring it is to have a partner out here.

Your body shakes from the wind pressure as your Protector screams out again, "You're not gonna make it!" But you remember to stop, be aware, and resume control. You keep your cool and enjoy the process. Struggle? Not a chance. That's all in the past.

Looking down you see the drop zone. You know where you're heading—your goal—and you're going to have fun on the way there.

I hold my altimeter up to your face. It reads 5,000 feet. We look at each other, smile, nod, and pull our rip cords.

You hear the distinctive *"phoomph"* of the canopy opening above you and a second later you are laughing out loud as you glide gently toward earth.

You yell out in triumph as you touch down, realizing that you have overcome your fears and done something new and exciting and full of joy.

You have become an Extreme Achiever, a person who sees the big picture life offers. You realize that the journey really is the destination. There are new goals to attain and you know how to reach them. Neutralizing struggle, redirecting fear, and staying focused are the habits you've learned. You see more opportunities and understand how every lesson connects to the greater whole of who you are and who you can be.

You understand a fundamental truth. On the earth or in the air, what's true in extreme sports is true in business and in life. If you really want to experience Extreme Success, you've got to take the leap.

Ready . . . set . . . go! It's time to jump into a life of Extreme Success!

How to Find a Personal Coach

⟶

The International Coach Federation's Coach Referral Service matches coaches with clients seeking their services. The system is accessible both on the Internet and by telephone. Hundreds of coaches worldwide list their practice and even link the listing to their homepage. The Coach Referral Service offers many benefits to anyone seeking a coach, including:

Internet Access

With its links to individual coaches' Web sites the International Coach Federation's Coach Referral Service is the premier source for those seeking the services of a coach. Many of the coaches listed in the Coach Referral Service have their own homepages, which can be accessed by simply clicking on the link provided, giving you more in-depth information to help you find the right coach for you. The Coach Referral Service allows you to browse the profiles of as many coaches as you like on the World Wide Web. Just visit the ICF's Web site at www.coachfederation.org, click on "Find a Coach," and begin viewing the qualifications and backgrounds of hundreds of coaches from around the world!

Toll-free Telephone Access

You do not need Internet access to use the Coach Referral Service. Call the ICF's toll-free number: 1-888-BE-MY-COACH (1-888-236-9262) or 1-973-239-7899. They will be delighted to assist you in finding the right coach.

About the Author

Rich Fettke has helped thousands of executives, entrepreneurs, and salespeople push their limits and expand their success without struggle. He has appeared on Fox TV News, Lifetime Television, and ESPN and has been featured in dozens of newspapers and magazines, including the *San Francisco Chronicle*, *Entrepreneur*, and *Self*. His diverse clientele includes IBM, Prudential, Morgan Stanley, and the United States Army.

In addition to his experience as a former CEO, Rich is also a record-holding extreme sports athlete and one of the country's top success coaches. He is past president of the Professional & Personal Coaches Association and was one of the first twenty-five coaches to receive the Master Certified Coach credential from the International Coach Federation.

As a professional speaker, Rich travels throughout North America to present his ideas to corporations and associations. He is also author and narrator of the audiotape program, *FOCUS: A Guide to Clarity and Achievement*.

Rich loves life in the San Francisco Bay Area with his wife, two daughters, and their dog, Zen.

For more information on Rich's speeches and workshops, please see page 283.

For his free online newsletter and success tips, E-mail: Subscribe@Fettke.com

Rich Fettke
1630 North Main Street, suite 352
Walnut Creek, CA 94596
Phone: 800-200-COACH (or) 925-945-1182
Web site: www.ExtremeSuccess.com
E-mail: Rich@Fettke.com

Rich Fettke
Inspirational Speaker

Encouraging people to push their limits and expand their success—without struggle—is Rich's gift. His energizing and humorous speaking style, combined with a practical "how-to" approach, has won rave reviews from corporations and associations throughout North America.

Rich leads his audiences to the path of success using idea-packed, interactive programs that provide the tools for greater personal effectiveness, not only at work, but in all areas of life.

SPEECHES AND WORKSHOPS INCLUDE:

- *Extreme Success*

- *The Courage for Change*

- *Make FEAR Your Friend*

- *Getting & Staying Focused*

If you would like to know more about these or other speeches, please call 800-200-2622 or 925-945-1182, or visit Rich's Web site at: www.ExtremeSuccess.com.